RIVER WILD

An Activity Guide to North American Rivers

RIVER WILD

An Activity Guide to North American Rivers

Nancy F. Castaldo

CHICAGO
REVIEW
PRESS

Library of Congress Cataloging-in-Publication Data

Castaldo, Nancy F. (Nancy Fusco), 1962–
    River wild : an activity guide to North American rivers for ages 7 to
9 / Nancy F. Castaldo.— 1st ed.
        p. cm.
    Includes bibliographical references and index.
    ISBN 1-55652-585-0
    1. Rivers—Study and teaching (Elementary)—Activity
programs—Juvenile literature. 2. Rivers—North America—Juvenile
literature. I. Title.
    GB1202.25.C37 2006
    372.8991—dc22

                                                2005022976

Cover and interior design: Monica Baziuk
Cover and interior illustrations: B. Kulak

© 2006 by Nancy F. Castaldo
First edition
Published by Chicago Review Press, Incorporated
814 North Franklin Street
Chicago, Illinois 60610
ISBN-13: 978-1-55652-585-8
ISBN-10: 1-55652-585-0
Printed in the United States of America

5   4   3   2   1

For my nephews, Gregory and Christopher, who have already crossed many rivers in their lives

Contents

Acknowledgments

MANY THANKS to everyone who shared his or her river expertise with me, including the riverkeepers: Alex Matthiessen, John Weisheit, Mary Lee Orr, Tim Gray, Danielle Droitsch, Sally Bethea, Jim Phillips, Meredith Brown, and Chuck Fredrickson.

Thanks to Jeffrey Rich for telling me about his salmon project, Victoria D. Quintero of the Gila River Indian Community, Debbi Michiko Florence for sharing the beauty of the Pacific Northwest, Hobbs Hosford for teaching me about "shooting the hooch," Rachel Wolff for sharing her inspiring Girl Scout Gold Award project, my unfailing team at Chicago Review Press that helps me create books to empower and inspire children, and my wonderful family and friends and Writers on Wednesdays (WOW) for their love and support.

Introduction

"In this sometimes turbulent world, the river is a cosmic symbol of durability and destiny; awesome, but steadfast. In this period of deep national concern, I wish everyone could live for a while beside a great river."

—Helen Hayes (1900–1993), resident of Nyack-on-the-Hudson

I grew up beside a river. Every day I walked to my bus stop with the view of the Hudson River in front of me. I moved to another house, even closer to the river. It brought the river directly into the view from my window. Later, I went to college beside the river. Every night I watched the sun's golden orange set across the shore. When I married I moved north, where the river is not as wide. I continue to cross the river regularly, ride the train against its shoreline, and kayak in its waters.

So many of us have similar experiences. Our life flows along with the rivers that are closest to us. We use their waters for energy, transportation, and recreation.

In *River Wild,* readers will be introduced to rivers in the United States, Canada, and Mexico. You'll investigate life along the riverbanks, the fast-flowing headwaters, and estuaries. You'll discover how rivers have shaped our history and the issues that are currently facing these waterways.

Facts will pop out in River Rapids sidebars, and ideas for more fun will appear in River Challenges sidebars. You'll find additional ways to explore rivers in the Resources section where you'll find recommended books, videos, and Web sites; a listing of related organizations and places to visit; a calendar of yearly events; a glossary of terms; and an index. My hope is that you'll discover a new frontier that you'll want to explore. So turn the page and start getting wild about rivers!

The River Highway

> "I started out thinking of America as highways and state lines. As I got to know it better, I began to think of it as rivers."
>
> —Charles Kuralt, from *The Magic of Rivers*

You may not think of America as rivers yet, but I hope by the end of this book you will. Rivers run through deserts and forests. They cut canyons and serve as boundaries for states and countries. These rivers link us together, run through our history, and are crucial to our future. They inspire us at every bend, feed us, and provide us with countless hours of amusement.

Take a look at a map of North America. Count the number of rivers you see. Before long you will realize it's almost impossible to count them all, and that hours might pass before you finish, if you finish at all.

Got River?

Are you thinking of America as rivers yet? Let's take another approach, using the picture on this page in the next activity.

What You Need

- Pencil
- Paper

What You Do

1. Think of all the different ways people and wildlife use rivers. Before looking at the picture write down as many as you can.

2. Now look at the picture. There are many different ways the river water in the picture is being used. How many did you already name on your list? Add the ones you didn't.

3. Did you see recreational uses? Transportation uses? Uses as a source of energy?

4. What are some of the things in the picture that might contribute to making the river unhealthy? Can you think of ways that those problems can be avoided?

Mallard Ducks

The Basics

Before we can think of America as rivers, we must determine what a river is. Let's start with the basics.

The dictionary defines a river as a large stream of water that flows in a bed or channel and empties into another body of water. But where do rivers begin? You might say they form right out of thin air. They begin high up in the clouds with a raindrop and the water cycle. When water droplets collide they become rain, sleet, snow, or hail, also known as *precipitation,* and fall to earth. Some of the rainwater falls right into a river. Some of it falls onto the ground and soaks into the soil. And some of it does not soak into the soil, but rather moves toward rivers, lakes, oceans, and streams as runoff. Eventually the water from the rivers, lakes, oceans, and streams becomes heated by the sun and *evaporates,* meaning it turns into vapor and rises into the air. As it rises it cools and becomes water droplets again. This is called *condensation.*

There is another path that precipitation takes when it falls to earth. Precipitation seeps into the soil and is absorbed by the roots of plants. After it is distributed throughout the plant, some of that water passes out through the pores in the leaves of the plant and evaporates into the air. This process is called *transpiration*. Just like the water that evaporates from the rivers, condensation follows.

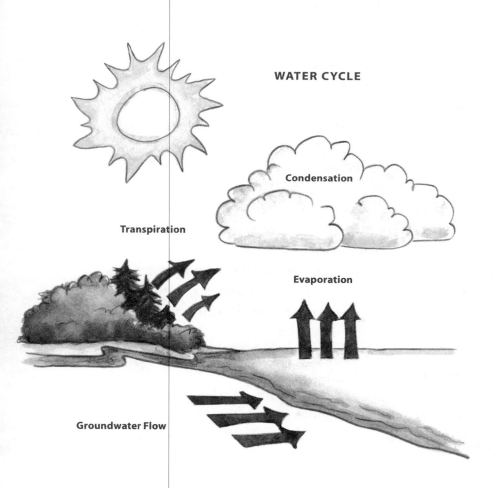

WATER CYCLE

Condensation

Transpiration

Evaporation

Groundwater Flow

Evaporation Experiment

You can see for yourself how the sun influences water evaporation with this simple experiment.

What You Need

- 2 glass or plastic beakers
- ¾ cup (177 ml) of water
- Grease pencil (so you can erase with a cloth and redo the experiment)

What You Do

1. Fill each beaker halfway with water. Mark the water lines with the grease pencil. Write the date next to the line.

2. Place one beaker in direct sunlight. Place the other beaker in a dark closet.

3. Visit the beakers after 24 hours. Mark the water line on each beaker. Write the date next to the line.

4. Visit the beakers the following day. Mark the water lines again and write the date next to the line. Now compare the beakers. Which one has less water? Did the beaker in the sunlight have more water evaporate? Since you've used a grease pencil, you can take a cloth, wipe the markings off the beakers, and redo the experiment. Do you get the same results?

River Headwaters

You've discovered how water gets into a river, but that is just part of the river's beginning. All rivers begin somewhere. The starting place or source is known as the *headwaters* of the river. The source could be a lake, a spring, or a few small streams that join together to form the larger river. (You'll find information about the headwaters of many major rivers in North America in the following chapters.)

The headwaters of a river are very important. They supply food and nutrients to the river, which help support the life in the water. Leaves that have fallen in the river become food for insects, which become food for fish. Everything is connected, just as it is in every environment. The fish, plants, and animals all depend on each other.

Headwaters also serve as their own ecosystems. These small, shallow waterways support a diversity of animals and plant life, some of which do not live in larger rivers. *Amphibian* populations—frogs, toads, salamanders, and newts, for example—are usually greater in the shallow headwaters than in the larger parts of the river where the water is deeper and the conditions (such as fast moving water) are less favorable for the survival of those kinds of animals.

The Food Chain Connection

A food chain follows a path where animals find food. For example a food chain will start with a plant, such as grass; the next link in the chain is the animal that eats the grass, such as a grasshopper. A toad might eat the grasshopper, forming the next link, and so on. A food web shows how various food chains are connected. Think about the creatures that live in and around a river. Can you think of food chains and webs that connect them?

It is very important to keep the river headwaters healthy. There are so many headwater streams that most people actually live close to one and can affect the health of these streams every day. You'll see as we explore North American rivers that when headwaters become unhealthy, the rivers they feed become contaminated. Can you think of something that might cause the headwaters to become unhealthy?

River Rapids

Let's look at one river as an example. The Hudson River in New York State begins high up in the Adirondack Mountains in a little pond called Lake Tear of the Clouds. As the lake fills and overflows, the water begins to head south as a small stream. As the stream flows through the mountains, water runs into it from other streams. Rain falls and snow melts. The stream becomes larger and the river is formed. The headwaters are in the mountains. The *watershed* is the large area of land where the water feeds the river. Finally, after 315 miles, the Hudson River meets the Atlantic Ocean. The area where the river meets the ocean is called an *estuary*.

Pollution, acid rain, logging, mining, building, and livestock grazing (which leads to contamination and an increase in river silt), are just some factors that might contribute to the poor health of headwaters.

The good news is that there are many things that can be done to restore and preserve headwaters. Conservationists are working with planners for better land use so that runoff from construction sites doesn't flow into streams and livestock grazing doesn't contaminate the water. Clean air laws help decrease acid rain. Conservationists are also working to monitor and minimize pollution discharges into streams.

Watersheds

A *watershed* is the area of land where all the water that drains off it or under it goes to the same place—the river. In turn, the rivers feed the lakes and the oceans. Watersheds come in all different sizes. They cross state boundaries and national boundaries. Even if we can't see a river from our homes, the water that falls around us will eventually end up in a stream or creek that will feed into a nearby river. These smaller bodies of running water are called tributaries.

Create Your Own River

Grab a friend and go outside to create your very own river.

What You Need
- 1 plastic drop cloth or tarp
- 2 buckets of sand
- 1 bucket of fist-sized rocks
- 1 bucket of mud
- Pitcher of water

What You Do

1. Place the drop cloth or tarp on the ground. Just like many rivers, your river is going to begin on a mountain. To make your mountain, pile up your rocks in the shape of a mountain on one side of the tarp.

2. Fill in the mountain by packing the sides of the rocks with the sand and mud. Does it look like a real mountain? Add more mud to the tarp around the base.

3. Gently begin pouring your pitcher of water to make it rain over the mountain. Watch carefully as the water creates a path or more than one path down the mountain. Does it form a deep channel at the top of your mountain? Does the channel widen as it flows down the mountain? Like all rivers, a certain amount of sand and silt flow into the river from the headwaters. Is that happening on your mountain?

4. Every river is different. You might want to re-create your mountain and try this experiment again to see what paths the water will take the second time.

River Research

Conservationists have many ways to study the health of a river and its tributaries. They roam the shore to spot birds and animals that visit the river and to see what the tides and currents leave at the waterfront. From the shoreline they can use a *seine* net to investigate the wildlife found in the waters. Fishing is another tool that gives researchers first-hand knowledge of the health and variety of fish species residing in the water.

Have you ever seen a river from the deck of a boat? Seeing a river from a boat gives you a whole different view of the river than from the shoreline. Not only do you have a different viewpoint, but you can feel the waves against the boat and you can look down into the water offshore. It also allows for other investigations such as the ones that follow.

The next time you are planning a boat ride, ask a grown-up to help you with some of these experiments that will help you further explore the river. With the following experiments you can investigate the river's temperature, depth, and water clarity.

Temperature Testing

Temperature is very important to the animals and plants that live in the river. Warm water has less oxygen than cold water, and a river that is unnaturally warmed will support fewer plants and animals than it did before. You'll see in other chapters how specific factors can raise or lower the temperature of a river and the resulting effect on the river's wildlife.

Here's how you can measure the temperature of a river using a weighted thermometer.

What You Need

- *A grown-up to assist*
- 10 feet (3 m) of string
- Scissors
- Pebbles, dime-sized
- Soda can, empty
- Can opener
- Thermometer (non-mercury with a looped end)
- Tape measure
- 2 permanent markers, different colors
- Paper to record temperatures
- Pen

TO MAKE THE WEIGHTED THERMOMETER

What You Do

1. Cut the string into two sections—one 2 feet (.6 m) long and one 8 feet (2.4 m) long.

2. Place the pebbles into the empty soda can to help it sink.

3. Ask a grown-up to make a small hole near the opening of the can using the can opener.

4. Thread the string through the loop of the thermometer. Place the thermometer inside the can.

5. Attach the thermometer to the can by slipping the string back through the hole in the can.

6. Using the can opener, have a grown-up make three sets of small holes evenly spaced around the top of the can so that the can stays upright when you lower it into the water.

7. Tie the long string to the can by weaving it through the holes. For the string that is outside and not wrapped around the can, use the tape measure to measure every 6 inches (15.2 cm) of the string and mark this using one of the colored markers. Mark every foot (.3 m) with the other marker.

TO USE THE THERMOMETER

What You Do

1. Lower the weighted thermometer into the water. Count the marks on the string to find out how deep you are lowering the thermometer.

2. Leave the thermometer in the water for five minutes.

3. Pull the weighted thermometer up quickly and carefully, keeping the tip submerged in the water. The can will be filled with water, so it will weigh more than before.

4. Read the thermometer.

5. Take the temperature at different depths at least an arm length apart, as indicated by your markings on the string, to see how it varies. Is it colder in deeper water or closer to the surface?

6. Record your temperature. Create a two-column table to record each depth you measure and each temperature you discover at that depth.

Did you find the temperature colder the deeper you dropped your thermometer? Did you see any fish when you were testing the water? Where were they? Were some swimming closer to the surface

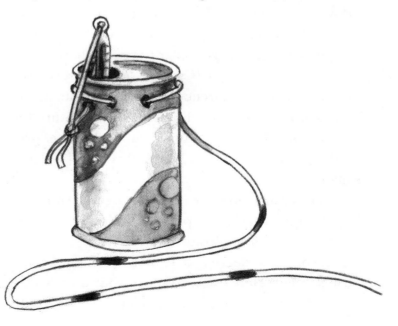

and others in the deeper water? What can you conclude from your findings? Write your conclusions under the table indicating the temperature at different depths.

Clear or Cloudy?

How clear is the water in the river? You can look down into the water from the deck of a boat or a dock and check this first hand. Can you see beneath the surface of the water? Can you see all the way to the bottom or is it cloudy? How far down can you see? You may not be sure. Sometimes the water is so clear that it almost looks shallower than it really is. Other times it is hard to see very far at all. That is why a biologist tests the clearness, or transparency, of the water with a Secchi (sek-EE) disk. The disk is used to measure the clarity of a body of water from the surface, providing a more precise measurement than just looking into the water.

The clearness of the river water can be affected by the amount of algae present, pollution, and suspended sediments from the bottom of the river. Transparency decreases as more of these factors are present. Here's how to make your own Secchi disk to test the water in your river.

What You Need

- *A grown-up to assist*
- White plastic lid 8 inches (20.3 cm) in diameter (or as close as possible)
- Black electrical tape
- Scissors
- Screwdriver
- 15 feet (4.5 m) of string
- 1 metal washer (such as those used in a kitchen sink faucet)
- Tape measure
- 2 markers, different colors
- Paper
- Pencil

What You Do

1. Stick black electrical tape to the lid to form two black sections opposite each other. Cut it to size so that it does not need to be folded over. (See the illustration below.)

2. Ask a grown-up to make a hole in the middle of the lid using the screwdriver.

3. Thread the string through the hole. Add the washer to the bottom and knot the string below the washer. The washer will help weigh the disk down so that it lies flat in the water.

4. Using the tape measure, measure every 6 inches (15.2 cm) of the string and use one marker to indicate this. Mark every foot (.3 m) of the string with the other colored marker.

5. Lower the disk into the water from a boat or dock until you are unable to see it in the water.

6. Raise the disk again until it reappears. Measure the depth of the string from the surface of the water to the

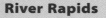

River Rapids

The Secchi disk was invented in 1865 by an astrophysicist, Father Pietro Angelo Secchi. He was a scientific advisor to the Pope, and the commander of the Papal Navy asked him to measure the clarity of the Mediterranean Sea. In April he used white disks to check the clarity. Many different sizes of disks have been used since that time, but the one most frequently used is a metal disk 8 inches (20.3 cm) in diameter painted with two black and two white sections.

nearest foot on the string. Record your measurement. Try taking the reading in other areas and at different times of the day. Record all your findings. What can you conclude? Write your conclusions on the paper under your readings.

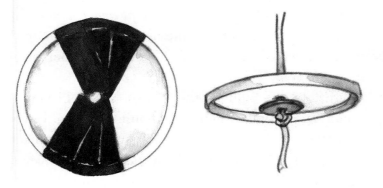

Settling Sediment

Here's a quick way to see how the minerals, leaves, and other items that flow into a river settle on the bottom to become sediment. Sediment can provide places for creatures to hide and things to eat, but it can also make the water cloudy and sometimes cause the river to be unhealthy. You'll also see how it can affect the clarity of the water.

What You Need

- 1 2-liter clear soda bottle
- Spoon
- Dirt
- Leaves
- Rocks
- Water

What You Do

1. Fill the bottle about ¾ full with water.
2. Spoon the dirt, leaves, and rocks into the bottle.
3. Cap the bottle and shake.
4. Notice how the water gets cloudy. Which items float to the top? Which sink to the bottom?

Think about these items in a river. Some would float down the river and others would settle on the bottom. What would happen if a lot of these items fell into a river? How could it change the river?

River Rapids

A lot of rivers in the southeastern part of the United States don't look as clear and clean as rivers in other areas. That's because the soil is mostly clay, and clay muddies the water.

The Riverkeepers

In the 1960s, when the conservation movement was growing in America, Robert Boyle wrote a book about the Hudson River in New York State called *The Hudson River: A Natural and Unnatural History*. In it he described the need for someone to work on behalf of the river. He called this person a riverkeeper.

In 1966, he founded the Hudson River Fishermen's Association, which helped build cases against industrial polluters. For almost 20 years, this organization worked to defend the Hudson River against polluters. In 1983 the association hired

John Cronin, a former commercial fisherman and congressional aide, to patrol the Hudson River full time. The riverkeeper program was born and continues with contributions from all over the country.

This riverkeeper program has led to the creation of more than 120 waterkeeper programs, which includes riverkeepers, coastkeepers, baykeepers, and streamkeepers to advocate on behalf of the waters they protect. They act as educators, scientists, coalition builders, investigators, spokespeople, and visionaries. They rely on many people to help them, including environmental experts, lawyers, local fishermen, and volunteers.

Waterkeepers use the Clean Water Act, which empowers private citizens to act as enforcement agents and public advocates, to collect evidence and file lawsuits against polluters. In this way, all of us can help monitor the health of our waterways.

We can watch for changes in the water or pollution being dumped into our streams and rivers. And because of the riverkeeper programs, we have someone to turn to for help. Every one of us has the right to clean air and clean water, and every one of us has the responsibility to help protect that right.

In the following chapters you'll hear from riverkeepers around North America. They come from various backgrounds. Some are fishermen, others

River Challenge
Find out if the river closest to your home has a riverkeeper.
Look at http://waterkeeper.org for help.

are lawyers, but they all share a love for and a commitment to the rivers they defend. You might find that you can help the riverkeeper in your area right now, or you might find that the riverkeeper job is something that interests you as a profession when you grow up. All riverkeepers and waterkeepers are listed in the Resources section.

Let's Get Wild About Rivers

Now that you know the basics, it's time to explore the rivers of North America. We'll start in the west, where there are fast-moving rivers that cut through canyons and provide energy to many Americans. Are you ready to ride the rapids? Let's go.

Ride the Rapids of the Western Rivers

2

> "To put your hands into the river is to feel the chords that bind the earth together in one piece. The sound of it at a distance is like wild horses in a canyon, going sure-footed away from the smell of a cougar come to them faintly on the wind."
>
> —Barry Lopez, from *River Notes: The Dance of Herons*

Western author Barry Lopez surely knows the rivers of this region. They do cut through canyons, as you'll see when we explore the Colorado, which cuts through the biggest of them all—the Grand Canyon. There are also many more rivers to discover, including the Sacramento and the San Joaquin. These rivers roar through canyons, meander through deserts, and spill out into the Pacific Ocean. Look on a map and follow their blue lines with your finger. We'll see how they have been explored, dammed for power, and how even nature has contributed to making rivers unhealthy.

River Discovery

Schoolteacher, naturalist, and former army officer John Wesley Powell led an expedition of 10 men on the Colorado River and its major tributary, the Green River, in 1869 to explore and chart the waters. At that time it was still a wild unexplored river in the heart of the Old West. There was only one bridge crossing the Green River, at Green River, Wyoming.

When they set out in four boats they had no idea what to expect from the river. Sometimes they were able to cover miles in a day as they sailed with the current, but other days the river waters were difficult to paddle through and they covered only a few yards. Sometimes their small boats coasted along, while other times the crew would need to row through slow waters, and still other times they would be bounced and whirled in the wild river. They suffered physically from the hot sun and long hours.

When they finally reached the point where the Green River meets the Grand River and forms the Colorado River, they still had not reached the Grand Canyon. They found the Colorado waters faster and the rocks bigger. The canyon walls soon became higher as they eventually entered into the Grand Canyon.

Only 5 of the original 10 members of the expedition completed the nearly 1,000-mile (1609-km) journey to the mouth of the Virgin River, which is now under the man-made Lake Mead. The men who completed the expedition had not been heard from for three months and were presumed dead.

The end of their expedition marked a change in the Colorado River's history. It was no longer just a wild river of legends and myths. It had now been explored and was soon to become the greatest source of irrigation water and electrical power in the American Southwest.

The Colorado River

The headwaters of the Colorado River, or *Red River* as it is named by the Spanish, are located high up in the Rocky Mountain National Park at an elevation of just over 9,000 feet (2743 m). It flows southwest toward the Gulf of California and the Pacific Ocean. Along the way it drops in elevation and cuts through the Grand Canyon. When it reaches the Grand Canyon at Lees Ferry, it has flowed to a lower elevation of just over 3,000 feet (914 m). By the time the river completes its journey through the canyon it drops another 2,000 feet (609 m).

This majestic river lies in one of the most visited national parks in the country. Even though people flock to it to see its beauty, it has been nominated year after year as the most endangered river by the American Rivers organization. The American Rivers organization studies the health of our rivers and compiles a list every year of the rivers that are unhealthy and in danger of becoming so unhealthy that they cannot support any life. Problems with pollution, high salt content, mercury, and temperature have contributed to the river's decline. How could this happen to the beloved Grand Canyon's Colorado River?

River:	**Colorado**
Length:	1,450 miles (2,333.5 km)
Distinction:	Cuts Grand Canyon
Major Tributaries:	Gila, Salt
Cities Served by River:	Phoenix
Riverkeeper:	Yes
Average Depth:	20 feet (6.1 m)
Watershed:	242,000 square miles (626,777 sq km)

Being a major tourist destination has not protected the Colorado River from the other industries that use and impact it. Coal-burning facilities producing power nearby have contributed to the high mercury levels in the river, a problem that exists in many of North America's waterways near these types of facilities. Mercury is a toxin that can be found naturally, but becomes more of a problem when it is released by unnatural sources, like coal-burning plants. It goes into the river and eventually, through the food chain, ends up in fish. If we eat the fish, we also eat the mercury, and it takes close to a year for it to leave our bodies. It is especially dangerous for babies and pregnant women because mercury tends to settle in the baby's brain and can be harmful.

In addition, an abandoned Atlas Corporation uranium mill on the Colorado River's bank in Moab, Utah, has led to 110,000 gallons (416,395 l) of radioactive groundwater seeping into the Colorado daily. Early in 2005, the U.S. Environmental Protection Agency declared the U.S. Department of Energy's plan to leave 12 million short tons (10,886,216 metric tons) of radioactive waste near the Colorado River near Moab "environmentally unsatisfactory." Environmentalists are working diligently to hasten this cleanup.

Not all of the Colorado River's problems are caused by humans. The river's landscape is quickly eroding. *Erosion* is a natural process by which land is worn away by wind or water. As it erodes, naturally occurring salts in the rocky soil are dissolved into the river, creating a very high salt concentra-

River Rapids
If you look out over the Grand Canyon you will see one of the best examples of erosion in North America. It is as if the different layers of rock that you see in the canyon walls are part of a large layer cake and the Colorado River is the knife that is cutting it.

tion, or *salinity,* level. The higher the concentration of salts in the water, the less fit it becomes for drinking and the more damaging it is to plants and animals. An estimated nine million tons of salt flows down the Colorado River every year past Lees Ferry, which is the dividing point between the Upper Colorado River Basin and the Lower Basin. A river basin is the land area where the water drains into the river.

Salty Water Experiment

The Colorado River's salinity level has changed the ecosystem drastically. Try this experiment to compare what happens to plants in salty water.

What You Need

- 2 small fishbowls
- Spring water
- 2 freshwater aquarium plants
- Salt
- Paper
- Pen

What You Do

1. Fill each fishbowl with spring water. Add a plant to each and place in a sunny window.

2. Add 2 tablespoons (30 ml) of salt to the first fishbowl.

3. Use the paper and pen to create a table to record your actions and observations that occur immediately and that occur after a few days. Use the following table as a model to complete and chart your findings in this activity.

Date	Fishbowl	Amount of Salt Added	Observations
4/20	1	2 tablespoons	no immediate change
4/20	2	—	no immediate change
4/22	1	—	plant is wilted
4/22	2	—	plant has grown
4/22	1	2 tablespoons	
4/22	2	—	

4. After two days, check the plants. Is there a difference in their growth?

5. If not, add another 2 tablespoons of salt to the first fishbowl and check it again after two more days. How much salt can you add to the fishbowl before the growth of the plant becomes affected? Think about how high the salinity in the Colorado River must be to change the ecosystem there.

Colorado Riverkeeper John Weisheit

Colorado Riverkeeper John Weisheit was originally inspired to become a riverkeeper by his parents, who encouraged him to work for the National Park Service. He is a self-educated naturalist with a high school education and the author of *Cataract Canyon: A Human and Environmental History of the River and Canyon Lands* (see more in the Resources section). He helps protect this river, in part, by giving lectures on the history and biology of the canyon.

Weisheit loves his job defending the Colorado River because of the natural beauty of the river and its surrounding canyon. But he is worried by the number of dams and other diversions in the river that seriously threaten the native fish population and the many birds and animal species, such as the otter, muskrat, southwest willow flycatcher, and yellow-billed cuckoo. He worries that if these issues aren't addressed soon, the river will become sterile, meaning it will be unable to support any life, and the ecosystem will crash.

The riverkeeper brochure for the Colorado River encourages kids to reduce water and energy use, help recruit adults to aid in working on the restoration of the Colorado River, and advocate the repeal of laws that do not support the river's restoration. Go to www.livingrivers.org to find out more about how you can help save the Colorado River.

Anatomy of a Dam

The Glen Canyon Dam rises over 700 feet (213 m) to block the flow of the Colorado River. Before the construction of the dam, the river carried 500,000 tons (508 million kg) of silt and sediment every day

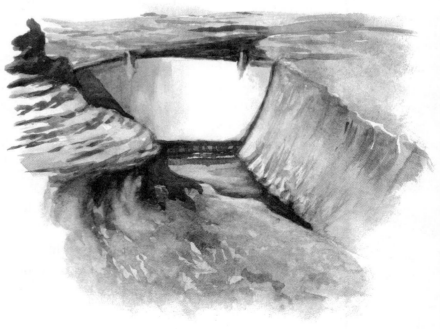

through the Grand Canyon. The primary reason for building the dam was to prevent the silt from building up behind Hoover Dam on the other side of the Grand Canyon, at the head of Lake Mead.

The Glen Canyon Dam was constructed with five million yards of concrete. A normal truck holds about 10 yards—can you imagine the number of trucks it would take to deliver five million yards? Behind this great wall is Lake Powell, which stores enough water to meet the needs of almost 30 million families each year. Lake Powell is one of the largest man-made reservoirs in the world. Its water is used for drinking and recreation.

About three million people visit the dam and Lake Powell each year. Those visitors spend an estimated $500 million annually in the nearby communities. The money helps support the economies of those communities.

Unfortunately the dam has damaged the ecology of the Grand Canyon. Before the dam was constructed, flash floods would occur that would rinse clean the sand and vegetation from the walls of the canyon and deposit fresh sand along the beaches, which provide a habitat for the wildlife of the canyon. That doesn't happen anymore.

The temperature of the Colorado River water has dropped drastically since the dam was built. The water flowing through the dam is coming from

River Rapids

Dams provide *hydroelectricity*, which is electricity created by waterpower. Water behind the dam can be released through water wheels called *turbines*, which turn generators that produce electricity.

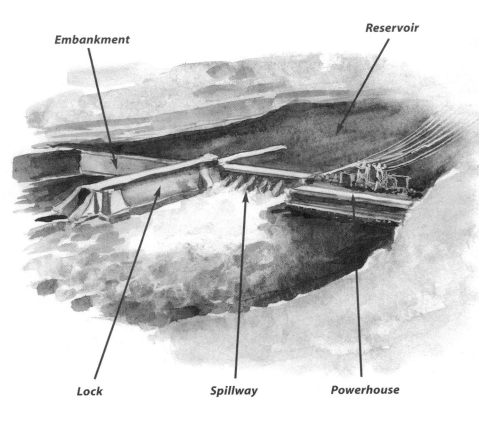

Embankment

Reservoir

Lock

Spillway

Powerhouse

200 feet below the surface of Lake Powell, where there is little sunlight, making it much colder than it would normally be. Before the dam was built, the water would get as warm as 80°F (26°C), but now it remains an average of 42°F (5°C). This drastic drop in temperature has caused some of the native fish that prefer warmer temperatures to become extinct and still others to become endangered.

River Rapids

The rainbow trout is a nonnative species of fish that was introduced into the Colorado River by humans. It thrives in the cold water. Many people who fish in the Colorado River and like to eat trout enjoy its healthy population. So what's so bad? Well, nonnative species compete with native fish to survive. The native fish, which are important to the river's food web, are usually the ones to suffer. The humpback chub is one of the native fish that once thrived in the river's warm, muddy water. Now there are barely 1,000 of them left. The chub is endangered, but there is still time to save it. Unfortunately the Colorado pike minnow, razorback sucker, bonytail chub, and roundtail chub are already *extirpated,* or regionally extinct.

Build Your Own Dam

There are roughly 75,000 dams greater than six feet wide in the United States, and tens of thousands more in smaller rivers and streams. While they can provide society with much needed power, water storage, irrigation, and flood control, they also damage our rivers.

Sometimes dams outlive their usefulness and their ecological costs start to outweigh their benefits. That's when they need to be removed. American Rivers is one organization helping communities remove harmful, unnecessary dams, through their "Rivers Unplugged" campaign. Many dams have already been removed and many more are in the process. In fact, 56 dams were slated for removal in 11 states in 2005.

While many dams need to be removed, many also need repair, and still others are being built. Here's your chance to be an engineer. Try your hand at building and testing your own dam.

What You Need
- *A grown-up to assist*
- ½ gallon (1.9 l) milk carton
- Scissors
- 8 craft sticks
- Newspaper

- Wood glue
- Pottery clay
- Assorted sticks, gravel, and dirt
- Water

What You Do

1. Cut the top of the milk carton just below the fold, and cut out one entire side of the carton.

2. Ask a grown-up to cut the craft sticks in half with scissors.

3. On a tabletop covered with newspapers, glue the craft sticks together side-by-side to form the dam wall. Let dry.

4. Place the carton on the table so that the cut-away side is facing up. Construct the dam by gluing the wall to the bottom of the milk carton in the center. Let dry.

5. Build up your dam by adding a triangular piece of clay against the outer side of the stick wall you have created.

6. Add sticks, gravel, and dirt over the clay layer. These materials are known as *riprap* in a real dam. You might need to mix more clay with these materials to help them stick to the dam.

7. Press firmly on the dam to make sure all the different layers are tightly attached.

8. Let your dam dry for a week. After it is dry, it's time to test it. Pour water slowly behind the dam. Can the water get through or is your dam holding it back?

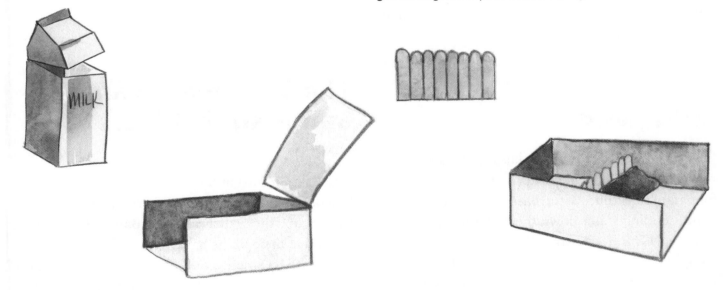

Save the River

There are three parts of the mission to save the Colorado River—conservation, preservation, and restoration. You can help the Colorado River from wherever you live by telling your friends and family about the problems it is currently facing. If more people know and care about the issues facing the river, there is a greater chance the Colorado River and Grand Canyon will survive.

You can also find out about the dams in your region. Are there any dams near you that are being built, repaired, or are in the process of being removed? Check out the American Rivers' "Rivers Unplugged" campaign in the Resources section for more information. Become an expert about dams and you can make a difference.

In the News!

On November 20, 2004, officials reported a plan to release a controlled flood on the 21st by opening four giant steel tubes at the base of the Glen Canyon Dam, sending water down the Colorado River and into the Grand Canyon. Environmentalists had complained for years that the Colorado River below the Glen Canyon Dam was washing away natural sediment in the Grand Canyon, wiping away beaches and native fish and plants. The flood would give the dam a chance to fix some of the problems it had caused in the canyon. The dam has trapped natural sediment for years, but the flood would allow it to flow freely for 90 minutes. Scientists estimated that 800,000 metric tons of sediment would be stirred up when the waters were released.

After the flood, scientists were optimistic that their plan was a success and a lot of sediment had returned to the river. A group of researchers rafted down the river and reported that the sediment had turned the river "velvety chocolate and red," a very positive sign.

The Sacramento and San Joaquin Rivers

Rather than start at the headwaters of these rivers, let's take a look at the point where these rivers meet the ocean, the San Francisco Bay in California, and trace their paths back.

The Sacramento and San Joaquin rivers flow into the north end of the San Francisco Bay. Following their paths back, we find that the two rivers meet near Pittsburg, California, before they flow west into the San Pablo Bay and then into the San Francisco Bay. If we trace their paths before they meet, we find that before reaching the bay, the Sacramento River is joined by the Butte Creek and the Feather River outside Sacramento. It flows west of Chico, and through Red Bluff and Redding, California. We then find the river dammed at Shasta Lake. The water feeding into the lake, the headwaters of the river, originates from snowmelt on Mount Shasta.

The San Joaquin River headwaters can be found high in the Sierra Nevada. The southern part of the basin between the Sierra Nevada and Coast Range is known as the San Joaquin Valley.

Like many rivers in North America, these two start out in higher elevations, and wind their way to the ocean. On the way, more streams and creeks join them to increase their size and flow.

River: San Joaquin

Length: 350 miles (563 km)

Distinction: Flows north to the Sacramento River

Major Tributaries: Stockton, the Mokelumne, Tuolumne, Merced, and Fresno

Cities Served by River: Fresno

American Heritage Designated Rivers: No

Riverkeeper: No

River: Sacramento

Length: 320 miles (514 km)

Distinction: Longest river in California

Major Tributaries: Pit River, Feather River, and American River

Cities Served by River: Sacramento

American Heritage Designated Rivers: No

Riverkeeper: Yes

Watershed: 27,000 square miles (69,929 sq km)

Gold Fever and the American River

In 1848 there was a discovery on the American River, which flows into the Sacramento, that forever impacted the West. In January, James Marshall discovered gold nuggets in the river. Marshall had been sent by John Sutter to build a sawmill to provide lumber for Sutter's ranch. Marshall and Sutter decided to keep the gold news quiet, but within months word eventually got out.

Still, there was no stampede to the American River to search for gold. It wasn't until a newspaperman by the name of Sam Brannan thought that this discovery could make him a very rich man that the rush began. Sam Brannan never panned for gold—instead he decided to buy up every pick ax, shovel, and pan in San Francisco. Then he stood out on the street with a bottle of gold dust and shouted out about the discovery. The prices for his equipment were promptly raised. The metal pan that sold for just $.20 rose to $15. Brannan made a fortune selling the shovels and other gold panning equipment in just nine short weeks. The American River region and the rest of the west grew quickly, never to be the same again. And it all started in the waters of the American River.

Pan for Gold

Gold isn't just found in the west. It's actually been found in all 50 states. So no matter where you live you can try your hand at panning for gold. You might be lucky and find some gold, or just find a new stream to wade in. For tips on the best places to pan for gold in your area, check out local rock and gem clubs or prospecting clubs. Look at Mama's Minerals at www.mamasminerals.com/learnmoreclubs.html for a listing of clubs by state.

What You Need

- Gold pan or shallow pie pan
- Tweezers
- Paintbrush
- Small bottle with tight-fitting lid

What You Do

1. With the pan, scoop up some sediment from the riverbank into your pan. Top it off with some stream water.

2. Carefully keep the pan slightly submerged in the stream and begin swirling the pan in a circular motion, letting the lighter sediment wash back out of the pan and into the stream.

3. Move aside any larger rocks and look at what's left in your pan.

4. Do you see any shiny, yellow material? Carefully remove any gold you find with the tweezers or paintbrush and place it in your bottle.

Color It Gold

Gold is naturally a soft metal. In order to make gold jewelry, it is often added to harder metals, like silver, to make it stronger. Gold jewelry is classified with a "karat code." The word *karat* comes from an Arabic word meaning "bean seed" because years ago, beans were used to weigh the gold. Gold that is 24K represents 100 percent pure gold, 18K denotes 75 percent pure gold, 14K is 58 percent pure, and 10K is 42 percent pure. Silver, zinc, and copper are usually mixed with the gold and help determine the final color of the gold jewelry. White gold jewelry, for example, tends to be mixed with white metals, such as palladium and nickel, which bleach the yellow gold to white. Increasing the amount of copper to gold will lead to a pink-tinged gold, called rose-colored gold. It's like mixing paint!

What You Need

- Yellow and white clay

What You Do

1. Divide your yellow and white clay into three equal pieces of each. Pretend the yellow clay is the gold and the white clay is the palladium metal that you want to mix.

2. Take one piece of yellow and one piece of white clay and mix them together with your hands until they form a new color. That would create a piece of gold very close to 14K. What color did you make?

3. Take another ball of yellow clay and add half of the last ball of yellow clay to it. Now add half of a ball of white clay to it. Is the finished ball of clay closer to 18K or 10K? If you picked 18K, you are right. The ball has 75 percent gold and only 25 percent of the other metal.

4. See if you can make other combinations.

Sacramento River Riparian Zone

The riparian zone of a river is the land extending out from the banks of the river. The riparian zone of the Sacramento is relatively flat and is bordered by the Sierra and Coast mountain ranges. It is made up of gravel bars, which are mounds of gravel, forests, and orchards. The soil is very rich and good for agriculture in the region, which includes rice fields and walnut, almond, and prune orchards. The Sacramento River Riparian Habitat Program is an organization that is working to ensure that the remaining riparian habitat is preserved and that management is in place to address the local agricultural community and protect it from development or overfarming, which would alter the habitat. The organization is also trying to reestablish a continuous riparian ecosystem along the river. Find out more at www.sacramentoriver.ca.gov.

Kids Make a Difference

Sometimes it is difficult to see how to help our rivers get healthy and how to protect species that are in trouble, but there are solutions. Teacher Jeffrey Rich at the Shasta Union Elementary School in northern California found a way for his students to make a difference in the Sacramento River.

Their school is located near Middle Creek, which feeds into the Sacramento River. For 50 years there hadn't been any salmon in the Sacramento River or the creeks that flowed into it due to the change in the flow of the river and pollution. Fortunately some of the river's problems had been addressed, but salmon were still not present.

Jeffrey Rich took his students to a fish hatchery and picked up a group of salmon eggs to raise. Since salmon prefer cold temperatures, the class kept the eggs in a tank in a refrigerator. The students became salmon experts. For example, they learned about a natural enzyme that weakens the eggshells when the young are ready to hatch. The tiny salmon then wiggle out of their shells. Young salmon have yolk sacs, full of nutrients, attached to their bellies. As they get older, the sacs shrink and they begin to look more like their parents.

When the sacs of these fish shrunk, the class knew it was time to release their baby salmon into Middle Creek. They hoped that the fish would swim about 3 miles (5 km) down the creek and into the Sacramento River. From there they would have to swim 200 more miles (320 km) to the ocean.

When the salmon matured, ready to lay their own eggs, they would swim back up the Sacramento River and into Middle Creek to lay their eggs.

The fourth and fifth grade students would have to be patient and wait. It takes between two and five years for salmon to mature. The class moved on, but that didn't stop them. For the next three years, Jeffrey Rich's classes raised and released more salmon. The older students stayed involved and helped the younger students when it came time to release each new group of young salmon.

So, do you think the salmon came back? They sure did! So with the help of a teacher and these young conservationists, after 50 years, salmon returned to Middle Creek.

This program continued for years. Now, over 10 years later, Jeffrey Rich says the salmon population is still up and running. "It's great to have some good news coming out of the environment."

River Challenge

You've seen how kids can make a difference with a species in their local river. Find out if there is a program like this in your area. Is there a way that you can join in or start your own? Check out your local land conservancy or similar conservation organization. They are just a phone call away!

Heading North

It's time to travel to the Pacific Northwest now, to a land where salmon is king and rivers flow through old forests and high mountains. Turn the page and come along!

The Great Rivers of the Northwest

"We call upon the waters that rim the earth, horizon to horizon, that flow in our rivers and streams, that fall upon our gardens and fields, and we ask that they teach us and show us the way."

—Chinook Blessing

The Chinook are Native Americans who inhabit the Pacific Northwest. In ancient days they lived along the Columbia River. They did not need to farm like many other Native Americans. The rivers, ocean, and forests provided them with plenty of food to harvest. Salmon were abundant. They swam from the ocean into the rivers to lay their eggs, many traveling 2,500 miles (4,023 km). The Chinook created fences from the tree saplings and channeled the fish into the nets of their fishermen. All members of the tribe helped to dry and smoke the fish, which they ate during the winter months.

Salmon Trap Game

Before we continue to explore the land of rivers and salmon in the Pacific Northwest, let's play a game that will bring the fishing fence to life.

What You Need
- 8 or more friends
- Large open area to play

What You Do

1. Choose a person to be the "salmon" and have the rest of your friends join hands to form the "fishing fence."

2. The fishing fence moves around and tries to catch the moving salmon.

3. When the salmon is caught, a new salmon is picked and the first joins the fishing fence to continue the game.

Can you imagine a fence in a river? Do you think that any other fish were caught by the fence the Native Americans used long ago? What are other ways to catch fish?

River Rapids

The Chinook believed that salmon were people who had left a magic village under the sea to provide food for others. For this reason the bones of the first salmon of the season to be caught were always returned to the river in a ceremony with the belief that they would be reborn as salmon-people when they reached the ocean.

The Columbia River

The source for the Columbia River is high up in the Canadian Rockies. In a clear mountain lake known as Columbia Lake, it begins its 1,200-mile journey to the Pacific Ocean. The Native Americans called this river *Nchi-wana*, or Big River. They relied on the river for survival. The Native Americans respected the river—they didn't pollute it or change its character—and lived in harmony with it and its wildlife.

This river has witnessed many changes in the name of progress over the last 200 years. By 1883 there were 40 salmon canneries on the river. They packed 35 million pounds (15.8 million kg) of cooked Chinook salmon in just one year! In 1884 the first pulp mill to make paper was built on the river, and by the 1930s dams were constructed for hydroelectric power. This growth took its toll on the ecosystem of the Columbia River. The logging and development along the river's shoreline and its tributaries destroyed the habitat and prevented the river from giving life to fish and wildlife.

The river now has 14 dams to provide electricity, flood control, and to open the river up to shipping. The dams caused salmon populations to decrease from 10 to 16 million in the 1900s to a

River:	**Columbia**
Length:	1,210 miles (1,947 km)
Major Tributaries:	Kicking Horse, Snake
Cities Served by River:	Portland, Eugene
American Heritage Designated Rivers:	No
Riverkeeper:	Yes
Watershed:	260,000 square miles (673,397 sq km)

River Challenge

Visit a fish counter and speak to the fishmonger about the salmon they carry. Find out where it comes from, and if it is farm raised or wild. Farm-raised salmon don't get a lot of room to swim and become more prone to disease. They can also get out of the farm and infect wild salmon. In addition, they often have high levels of mercury. You can write letters to supermarket chains and tell them you are concerned about the fish they carry.

current population of 200,000 to 300,000. This has also impacted jobs and towns in the region. The Columbia Riverkeeper organization is working hard to address these issues.

Columbia Riverkeeper Greg deBruler

After originally wanting to be a doctor or attorney, a windsurfing experience in 1986 changed Columbia Riverkeeper Greg deBruler's ambition. He asked himself about the water quality and realized that no one was keeping watch. He's been working as a riverkeeper since 1989. DeBruler didn't receive any special training to be a riverkeeper; he says that all you need is a caring heart. In his job he enjoys talking to children at schools about what they can do to help preserve rivers.

DeBruler is very concerned about the cleanup of the plutonium manufacturing sites around Hanford, Washington, and the Columbia River. Plutonium was created in a plant located on the shores of the river years ago by our government when it was manufacturing nuclear weapons. The waste from the manufacturing was dumped into tanks and then buried. The U.S. government doesn't want to clean it up, but the waste will kill the river—and all the plant and animal life in it—if the site is not cleaned up.

Kids can find out more about the Hanford cleanup at www.hanford.gov and about the Columbia River at the riverkeeper's Web site at www.columbiariverkeeper.org/page1.htm.

Columbia River's Majestic Multnomah Falls: A Legend

The second highest year-round waterfall in the United States, Multnomah Falls, drops 620 feet (188.9 m) from Larch Mountain in Oregon. Visitors travel the Columbia River Gorge Scenic Highway to see the falls, as well as the views of the river and its landscape along the way. This spectacular waterfall has inspired many throughout the centuries, including the Native Americans, who tell this tale of Multnomah Falls and Coyote.

LONG AGO when the world was young, and the birds and animals spoke to each other, coyote (ki-o-ti) was the most powerful of all the creatures. The Spirit Chief had given him the power to change the course of the Great River [Columbia] leaving Dry Falls behind.

Coyote had seen a beautiful girl in a village close to the spot where the Great Bridge joined the mountains on one side of the river with the mountains on the other side. The girl's father was the chief.

When he reached the place where water flowed under the bridge he changed himself into a handsome hunter. He went to the chief to ask for his daughter's hand in marriage. He gave the chief a great gift of skins to please him. The chief was pleased with the skins, but loved his daughter very much and decided that he would not trade her for a pile of skins. He told the hunter that he would have to win the heart of his daughter.

Every day the hunter brought a small gift to the maiden, but it did not win her heart. Then he thought that perhaps if he found the loveliest flower in the forest for her that she would be happy. He looked and looked all day for the prettiest flower for the maiden. When he had gathered a bunch, he brought them to her father.

"Chief, I have gathered these flowers all day for your daughter. Will she be pleased?" asked the hunter.

"You should ask my daughter what will please her," said the wise chief.

When the hunter presented the flowers to the beaufitul maiden and asked her what her desire was, she answered, "I would like a pool, where I can bathe and no eyes will be upon me."

With that the girl ran away. The hunter promised the chief that within seven suns he would build a pool for his daughter. The hunter then left to build the pool. First he made a great slash on the hills on the south side of the Great River, and lined it with ferns, trees, and other greens.

Next he hollowed out a pool at the bottom of the rock wall. He climbed back up and went into the hills where he made a stream. He sent the stream down the gash and into the pool below. As the water fell into the pool it sent up a mist to hide the pool from peering eyes. When he was finished he took the maiden and her father to see what he had made.

The maiden was very pleased. ❋

Love of a River Poetry Contest

Each spring the Columbia Riverkeeper holds the "Love of a River" poetry contest. The poems can be any length or style as long as they are about the Columbia River. They are judged in student and adult divisions. Check out the Columbia River-keeper Web site at www.columbiariverkeeper.org/riverpoetry.htm for the dates of the current contest and more information on submitting your own poem. It's the perfect way to celebrate the Columbia River!

The Yellowstone River

Originating in Yellowstone National Park, the Yellowstone River is the longest river in the state of Montana. Unlike the Colorado and Missouri rivers, the Yellowstone runs free of any major dams. It sustains many fisheries, cottonwood forests, and rural communities in Montana.

Fly-fishing is a big draw to the river. Fly fishermen construct flies, or lures, of fur, feathers, thread, and other materials and tie them to their hook instead of live bait, such as worms, to attract fish. The fishing rods they use are a bit lighter and longer than other rods.

The cold waters in the upper half of the river promote thriving populations of cutthroat trout, rainbow trout, large whitefish, and brown trout. The warmer waters of the lower half of the river, south of Billings, Montana, support healthy populations of walleye, catfish, and sturgeon.

Keeping the Yellowstone running free is the goal of regional conservationists. They know the future of this pristine river depends on controlling development and monitoring river use.

A River Runs Through It

"Eventually, all things merge into one, and a river runs through it. The river was cut by the world's great flood and runs over rocks from the basement of time. On some of the rocks are timeless raindrops. Under the rocks are the words, and some of the words are theirs. I am haunted by waters." ❧

Norman Maclean wrote about his memories growing up and fishing with his dad and brother on the Big Blackfoot River in Missoula, Montana, in his book titled *A River Runs Through It*. This story was made into a successful movie in 1992.

A lot of care went into making this movie to preserve Maclean's vision. Trout used in the movie were pond raised in Montana and kept in a specially aerated and cooled tank truck until their big moment in front of the cameras. No hooks were used, and no blood was drawn. A line was tied to each fish's lower jaw under the careful observance of the Montana Humane Society. None of the actors had ever fly-fished before. See the Resources section for more details about the movie.

Fly-Fishing Fun

Whether you are fly-fishing or just dropping a line into the water, you can have a lot of fun and learn even more about the fish that live in your river. After you catch them, you can even toss them back. This is called catch and release, and many fishermen do this because they catch fish only for sport. If you decide to eat the fish you catch, then only keep the fish that meet the posted fishing guidelines for size and quantity. Here's how to start.

What You Need
- *A grown-up to assist*
- Fishing rod
- Fishing reel
- Weights
- Hooks
- Bait or fishing lures

What You Do

1. Find out the fishing regulations in your area. Kids usually don't need a license to fish, but if the grown-up with you wants to fish, he or she must get a license. Ask at a local bait shop if lures or live bait work best in the river near you.

2. Find a spot to fish. It's fun to fish right off the shore. You can also fish from a dock or a boat. If you are fishing on a dock or boat, make sure to wear a life preserver.

3. You'll need to buy the right bait for the fish that are in the area. If you are fly-fishing, you will need the right lure. A good bait and tackle shop will help you select the right bait or lure.

4. Have a grown-up flatten the sharp barbs of your hooks that are meant to hold your fish firm on the hook so that you will easily be able to release any fish you catch.

5. Now you are ready to fish. Have a grown-up bait your hook. If you are on a dock or a boat you just need to drop your line into the water. If you are fishing from shore you need to cast your line into the river. Ask a grown-up to show you how the first few times.

6. Reel a little line in until you feel a little bit of pull on your line. That will keep your line taut so that you will easily be able to feel a fish nibbling at your hook.

7. If you feel a fish take your bait, jerk your line slightly so that you are sure your fish is planted on the hook. Then begin reeling your line in slowly. If you pull too fast, you might lose your fish.

River Rapids

Just like counting tree rings on a tree to find out its age, you can tell the age of a fish by counting the lines on the scales of the fish. Take a look at the fish you caught. Look at a scale under a microscope. You will see rings just like from a tree trunk. Look for areas where there is a crossover of lines. These crossover points represent years. Can you tell how old it is? For more information on finding out the age of fish using this method go to www.nps.gov/muwo/nature/fauna/salmon/age.htm.

Fish Scales

Fry Bread

Here's a recipe for fry bread made by the Blackfeet people of Montana. It's good with whatever you're having for dinner.

What You Need

- Measuring cup
- 3 cups flour (.7 L)
- 1½ tablespoons (22.5 ml) baking powder
- ¾ teaspoon (3 ml) salt
- 1¼ cups (296 ml) water
- Mixing bowl
- Wooden spoon
- Large baking pan
- Nonstick cooking spray

What You Do

1. Preheat oven to 350°F (176°C). Mix together the flour, baking powder, and salt.

2. Add the water gradually. If the dough seems too dry, add a little more water.

3. Knead the dough by pressing down on it with clean hands and pulling it until it is not sticky.

4. Spread the dough out on the greased baking pan so that it is about an inch (2.5 cm) thick. Bake for 35 minutes.

The Yukon River

Where does the Yukon start? It used to be thought that the Yukon River started at Hootalinqua, where the Pelly River joins what used to be called the Lewes River, but in 1999 a federal hydrologist determined that the source of the Yukon River is actually a stream fed by the Llewellyn Glacier at the south end of Atlin Lake in British Columbia, Canada.

Alaska's Other Rivers

The Yukon River is the dominant river in Alaska, but it's certainly not the only one. The 100-mile (161-km) long Charley River is often picked as the most spectacular of Alaska's rivers. Brooks River of Katmai National Park may be one of the most visited, because visitors can see bears fishing for salmon there.

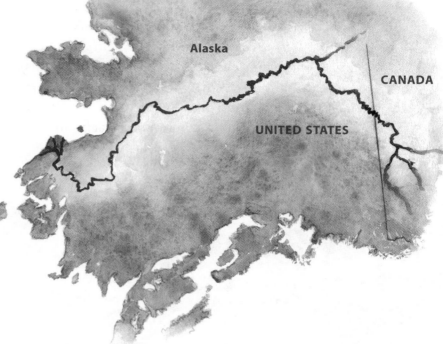

Alaska

CANADA

UNITED STATES

River:	Yukon
Length:	2,200 miles (3,540 km)
Cities Served by River:	Fairbanks, Fort Yukon, Dawson
Riverkeeper:	No
Watershed:	327,600 square miles (840,000 sq km)

Salmon-Munching Bears

Both brown bears and grizzlies live in Alaska—and they all love salmon. Brown bears are very large—they can weigh 860 pounds (390 kilograms) or more—and are mostly found in southwestern Alaska and along the coast of the Gulf of Alaska. They feed on spawning salmon there each summer.

Bear Catching Salmon

Grizzly bears live inland. Males average about 700 pounds (317.5 kg). They are cousins of the coastal brown bears, but are a little smaller because they eat less salmon and more plants. Fishermen sometimes meet up with bears along Alaska's rivers. Of course, if a bear wants a fish, the best advice is to let the bear have the fish.

River Rapids
Alaskan salmon average about 40 pounds (18 kg), but can weigh much more. The record holder was a whopping 97 pounds (44 kg)!

Salmon Survivor

It is very important that salmon populations remain healthy in all their native rivers. We know that we have to guard against housing and industrial development and pollution, but what about the bears? Bears eat a lot of salmon. Do they threaten the salmon population? Let's see.

What You Need

- Paper
- Pencil
- Calculator

What You Do

1. An average mature female Chinook salmon lays 8,000 eggs. Write down 8,000 on your paper.

2. Let's pretend that we know that ½ of those eggs will produce female salmon and the other half will produce male salmon. Draw two lines from the number 8,000 and write down 4,000 girls and 4,000 boys at the bottom of each line.

3. It takes salmon four years to mature and lay eggs. Let's draw another line from the 4,000 and write 4,000 × 8,000 because each of those 4,000 females will lay 8,000 eggs. Now it is time for your calculator. Ask a grown-up to help you multiply 4,000 by 8,000. How many new eggs do you have?

4. If you keep up this process you will find that after five generations of salmon you will have 2,048,000,000,000,000,000 (or 2 quintillion) eggs. Do you think the rivers can support all those salmon? It is important to see that there is a food chain that keeps all these populations in check. Bears are at the top of the food chain in Alaska, the salmon a bit lower. Find out what the salmon eat and the other links in the food chain that are necessary for all to have healthy populations.

Salmon Cycle

Salmon are *anadromous*, which means that they live in salt water, but return to the freshwater streams they were born in when they mature. Shad and the alewife are two other anadromous fish species. The opposite of this is *catadromous*. Species that are catadromous, like the American eel, spend most of their lives in freshwater and return to the sea to deposit their eggs, or *spawn*.

Some salmon travel thousands of miles to return to freshwater streams to spawn. Their journey back is a mystery. Do they follow the sun or

River Rapids

What do you think happens when a river is dammed and the fish can no longer continue on their journey to spawn? Often state departments of natural resources build fish ladders, also called fish ways or fish passes, and elevators for the migrating fish so that they can continue their migration. There are many different types of ladders. Each ladder is designed for a specific river. When the ladder is in place, the migrating fish can continue their journey without being halted by a dam.

stars? Do they know the water by the level of salinity, or temperature, or odor? Some people think that their migration is random. What do you think? Can you think of an experiment that might be used to determine how they arrive back in their freshwater rivers?

The Snake River

Named for the people who once lived in the desert surrounding the river, who marked their territory with sticks depicting a snake, the Snake River flows through Hells Canyon, the deepest gorge in North America, and forms the boundary between Idaho and Oregon. It was designated a National Wild and Scenic River in 1975.

The Snake River irrigates, or naturally waters, 3.8 million acres (1.52 million hectares) of land. It produces over 10 megawatt hours of electrical power. It's also a vacation paradise for fishermen, who find a variety of fish, including trout, catfish, and sturgeon, in the waters. Owls, hawks, falcons, and eagles make their home in the canyon around the river.

American Rivers Takes Action

American Rivers, the watchdog organization for all our rivers, is currently working hard to recover wild salmon and revive salmon-related jobs and economies. It is urging the government to write a strong Federal Salmon Plan that will help the Columbia and Snake rivers to recover wild salmon and steelhead to abundant, fishable levels and allow for the removal of the four lower Snake River dams. At that time the salmon will have sufficient population numbers to be able to support fishing for recreation and food. This will also benefit the local economy with increased tourism and commerce. You can learn more about this issue on the American Rivers Web site. See the Resources section for details.

Sailing South

Say good-bye to the salmon. We're heading to the rivers of the Southwest. We'll investigate the Rio Grande and the Brazos and Gila rivers. Who knows what we'll discover on this journey. Are you ready? Let's go.

Rivers of the Southwest and Mexico

"A river seems a magic thing. A magic, moving, living part of the very earth itself."

—Laura Gilpin from *The Rio Grande,* 1949

American landscape photographer Laura Gilpin was speaking about the Rio Grande in the quote to the left, but don't all rivers appear to have a little magic? I think she knew that. They seem to weave a tapestry across the earth, connecting people, mountains, and oceans. The Rio Grande is by far the most well-known and imposing river in this region, so that's where we'll begin our journey of river discovery.

The Rio Grande, or *Rio Bravo,* River

Javelina

The Rio Grande, or *Rio Bravo,* as it is called in Mexico, begins at 12,000 feet in the snowcapped San Juan Mountains and, with its tributaries, flows through the states of Texas, Colorado, and New Mexico in the United States and the states of Durango, Coahuila, Nuevo Leon, and Tamaulipas in Mexico. Close to 13 million people rely on its waters.

The Rio Grande/Bravo has received a great deal of attention. Many of its unresolved problems, including pollution, regional poverty, and economic issues, threaten the health of the river. The river basin has a fragile desert ecology. The basin has both dry, or *arid,* and moderately dry, or *semi-arid,* habitats. Rapid population and development growth in the region continues to affect the environment's natural balance.

It is important that there is collaboration between the governments of Mexico and the United States to relieve some of the problems facing this region. An agreement made in 1944 between the two countries provided for the distribution of the river's water, but during years of drought, the amount of water reaching the United States is often less than what the treaty established. Concrete channels and canals have helped the situation by clarifying the borders of the river, but the two countries must continue to cooperate to help solve many more problems facing the river.

River:	**Rio Grande**
Length:	1,885 miles (3,033 km)
Distinction:	Forms part of the border between Mexico and the United States
Major Tributaries:	Pecos
Cities Served by River:	Brownsville, El Paso, Laredo, Albuquerque
American Heritage Designated Rivers:	Yes
Riverkeeper:	No
Watershed:	185,000 square miles (479,148 sq km)

What's a Bosque?

Bosque is a Spanish word that describes a low-lying cottonwood forest adjacent to a river. Cottonwoods only grow well in land where their roots can reach moisture provided by underground water and where their seeds can germinate, or sprout, on bare moist soil. Because of this they are limited to areas with permanent water supplies, such as land near rivers.

There is a bosque on the banks of the Rio Grande. If you visit the bosque during the fall and winter months, you might see sandhill cranes, Canada geese, ducks, and occasionally a coyote, raccoon, or beaver. You might also spot another native, the great horned owl, the largest owl in North America.

The bosque has existed near the Rio Grande for over a million years, as evidenced by fossils of cottonwood and willow found in the area. The Native Americans who lived there over a thousand years ago used the bosque timber to build houses.

There is a myth that the Rio Grande bosque is in terrible health, but actually there are still major stands, or growths, of cottonwoods and willow. However, there are frequent fires in the bosque. Conservationists and communities have worked together to clear out burned trees, mulch the remaining stumps, replant, and restore the bosque to its original condition.

Big Bend National Park

One of the best places to explore the Rio Grande is at Big Bend National Park in Texas. It is named for the "big bend" in the river that is caused by the change in the flow of the river from southeast to northeast. The Rio Grande borders the Big Bend National Park for 118 miles (190 km).

Big Bend is home to more than 1,200 species of plants, 11 species of amphibians, 56 species of reptiles, 40 species of fish, 75 species of mammals, 450 species of birds, and roughly 3,699 species of

Visiting the Park

Big Bend is one of the largest and least visited national parks in the United States. It has more than 801,000 acres (324,153 hectares) and offers backcountry campsites and the Chisos Mountains Lodge for overnight visitors. Check out the National Park Web site at www.nps.gov/bibe/index.htm for more information on visiting this park.

insects. Some of those species are currently listed as endangered, including the black bear, peregrine falcon, black-capped vireo, and the Mexican long nose bat. The most well-known park resident by far is the mountain lion; in fact, Big Bend is mountain lion country!

There are more than 150 mountain lion sightings each year in the park. While mountain lions are crucial members of the wildlife community, as a top predator on the food chain, an encounter with a mountain lion is not advised. What can you do to minimize your contact? Don't hike alone. Avoid hiking at dawn or dusk when they are more active. Stay with a grown-up. Never run ahead on a trail.

Mountain Lion

If You Meet a Mountain Lion

1. Don't run away.
2. Have a grown-up pick you up so that you appear larger.
3. Wave your hands and shout.
4. Throw stones at the mountain lion if it begins to act aggressively.
5. Report lion sightings to a park ranger.

Mountain Lion Survival Shuffle

How would you do if you were a mountain lion in Big Bend National Park? Could you survive? Let's play and find out.

What You Need
- *A grown-up to assist*
- 10 to 12 friends

- 45 index cards
- Markers

What You Do

1. Write the word "Squirrel" (2 pounds [.9 kg]) on 15 cards, "Javelina" (55 pounds [24.9 kg]) on 10 cards, "Mule Deer" (150 pounds [68 kg]) on 3 cards, and "Rabbit" (4 pounds [1.8 kg]) on 14 cards.

2. The three extra cards are for mountain lion challenges. Mountain lions are the predators, or hunters, in this game. There are many things that can hamper a mountain lion's ability to hunt for its prey. Write one of the following sentences on each card.

- Twins born—find another 50 pounds (23 kg) of food for each
- Stepped on a cactus—miss 1 turn
- Broken leg—miss 2 turns

3. Now you are ready to start playing. Shuffle all the cards. The object of the game is to collect prey cards that total at least 100 pounds (45.3 kg). A mountain lion needs 100 pounds of food to live for two weeks.

4. Sit in a circle with the deck of cards in the middle. Everyone picks one card from the top of the deck. If you pick a prey card, put it face up in front of you. If you pick a challenge card, follow the directions on it.

5. Continue taking turns until all the cards are passed out. Look at your cards. Each player should add up the weight on his or her cards. Ask a grown-up to help with the math if you have trouble. How many weeks can each player survive in the park? Now pretend that there is a shortage of prickly pears for the javelinas to eat and they move out of the park. Remove all the javelina cards from your piles. How many weeks can you survive now? Which player can survive the longest amount of time in the park? Was there enough food for everyone? What happened to the mountain lion that broke its leg? Could it survive? Talk about other things you found out during the game.

Dig in a Box

Archaeologists can discover many things when they dig. They might find bits of pottery and buttons or other clues to help them learn about the people who left the objects behind. There are many places in the southwestern deserts that archaeologists have explored, including areas near the Rio Grande and other rivers. They've found many things, including items, known by researchers as *artifacts*, made by the Hopi Indians, such as *petroglyphs*. Would you like to be an archaeologist? How good are you at looking at clues? Get a big group of your friends or classmates together and see if you can learn about each other in this dig.

What You Need

- *A grown-up to assist*
- 5 or more friends or classmates
- A shoebox for each person
- Personal items
- Paper
- Pencil

What You Do

1. Each person should take the box home. Write your name on the bottom of the box.

2. Place items in the box that are meaningful, such as favorite toys, books, jewelry, and shoes. What do these items say about you? Make sure that you don't include any items in the box that have your name on them.

3. Take the box to your meeting place or classroom. Put all the boxes in a separate area. Have a grown-up assign a number to each box.

4. Everyone should look at all the other boxes except his or her own. Look carefully at the items in the box. Can you guess who owns the box? Write down the number and your guess on your paper. List the clues that make you think you know the owner of the box.

5. Take turns looking at the different boxes. When everyone has finished, ask the grown-up to read out the numbers and the owners of each box. How many did you get right? Were some easier to guess than others? Why? Remember, archaeologists are looking at clues from a very long time ago. What are some things that might help them with their investigation?

6. Look at the boxes you didn't identify correctly. Look at the clues you wrote down and think about how you either didn't interpret them correctly or how you misidentified a clue that led you to conclude the wrong owner.

Stepping Back in Time

The first people to inhabit the Rio Grande watershed were Native Americans, who hunted and farmed there. The land attracted both American and Mexican farmers and ranchers by the year 1900. While most of the United States was entering the industrial age with an increase in manufacturing, the area of the Rio Grande was still a frontier community. The Mexican Revolution of 1910, a violent struggle to overthrow dictator Porfirio Díaz, brought a lot of distress to the region as bandits and raiders attacked settlers on both sides of the river. Many Mexicans fled to the north side of the river for safety. The United States sent the army to establish camps along the river to defend the border. Camp Santa Helena was one of those camps and is now in the corner of Big Bend National Park.

Learn a Little Spanish

The Rio Grande may form a political boundary between Mexico and the United States, but nature does not recognize political borders. Wildlife moves from one side to the other. There are also many families that have members living on each side of the Rio Grande/Rio Bravo. The people in this region speak both Spanish and English. Here's how you can start learning a little Spanish.

What You Do

1. Let's start by learning how to say hello in Spanish. *Hola* (oh-lah). How about another greeting? *Buenos dias* (BWEH-nos DHEE-ahs) means good day.

2. Say the numbers aloud: 1, 2, 3, 4, 5, 6, 7, 8, 9, 10. Now try them in Spanish: *uno* (OO-no), *dos* (dose), *tres* (trace), *quatro* (KWAT-ro), *cinco* (SINK-o), *seis* (saze), *siete* (SEE-yet-eh), *ocho* (OCH-o), *nueve* (NEW-eh-veh), *diez* (DEE-ace).

3. How many legs does a mountain lion have? How many fingers do you have? Can you answer in Spanish?

4. Let's try something else. What is your name? You would answer in English, my name is _____. In Spanish the question is *¿Cómo te llamas?* (COMO te YA-mas?) You would answer in Spanish, *me llamo* (MAY YAH-moe) _____ (add your own name).

5. See if you can learn some more Spanish words. Look in the Resource section for some Web sites to help you.

The Brazos River

The longest river in Texas, the Brazos flows southeast through Texas to the Gulf of Mexico. The full name of the river in Spanish is *Los Brazos de Dios* (los BRA-zos day DEE-os), meaning, "the arms of God." There is a legend that Francisco Vazquez de Coronado and his men were wandering in the region dying from lack of water when the Native

River: Brazos	
Length: 800 miles (1,287 km)	
Cities Served by River: Waco, Lubbock	
American Heritage Designated Rivers: No	
Riverkeeper: No	

Americans guided them to a small stream that the men named Brazos de Dios. There are two other legends about the naming of the river. One tells the story of a ship that had exhausted the sailor's supply of drinking water. Parched with thirst, the sailors came across a muddy stream. They followed it and came across a wide river of fresh water. They were overjoyed and christened the stream Brazos de Dios.

The last legend tells about a drought that had spread to the Spanish miners in the region. The men found a Native American village and a stream of freshwater, which they named Brazos de Dios.

You may choose to believe one of these stories or none of them. Can you make up a tale that explains the name of your local river?

The Residents of Brazos Bend State Park

Much of the 4,897-acre (1,982-hectacre) Brazos Bend State Park is located in the Brazos River floodplain. Some of the park includes upland coastal prairie. There are mossy live oaks and bottomland hardwoods in the park, as well as some bayous and lakes. Head to the park in the spring for prime birdwatching. More than 279 species of birds have been sighted in this park. There are also 21 species of amphibians and reptiles in the park, and 23 species of mammals.

American Alligator

The American alligator (*Alligator mississippiensis*) makes its home in lakes, swamps, and rivers in the southern United States and Central America. Have you ever seen one basking on a riverbank? Alligators look like large lizards; in fact the word *alligator* actually comes from the Spanish word *el lagarto*, which means "the lizard." Just like lizards, alligators are reptiles. They are North America's largest reptile and are members of the crocodile family. They've been on this earth for millions of years.

River Challenge
Tales about the names of places, lakes, mountains, and rivers are fun to hear. Find out some local legends for the names of places where you live. Ask your local librarian to help you find some in the library. Make up some of your own.

American Alligator

With the large amount of alligators that can be spotted in rivers and swamps in Texas, Florida, Louisiana, and Georgia, it's hard to believe that their population was ever in danger of extinction, but in fact it was. They were hunted for their hides. Now their major threat is loss of habitat and encounters with people.

Alligators are important members of their ecosystem. When they nest they help create a substance called *peat*, which consists of roots and fibers in different stages of decomposition. Some animals, like the Florida red-bellied turtle, use this peat to nest themselves. Like all members of an ecosystem food chain, alligators serve a vital link.

Measure Up to an Alligator

Adult alligators can reach up to 18 feet (5.5 m) in length. Let's find out how you measure up to an alligator.

What You Need
- Yardstick
- Masking tape

What You Do

1. Place a piece of masking tape on the floor. Lay the yardstick down in front of the tape. Continue measuring with the yardstick until you reach a distance of 18 feet (5.5 m). Place another piece of tape at the end to mark the length of an alligator.

2. Lie down with your feet on the masking tape. Have a friend use the yardstick to measure you. Place a piece of tape on the floor to mark your length.

3. How much longer is the alligator? Male alligators can weigh 450 to 600 pounds (204 to 272 kg). How much do you weigh? You can see why it is not a good idea to get too close to an alligator. They are much bigger and eat just about anything. It is best to look at them from a distance.

Prickly Pear Cactus Jelly

Prickly pear cactus is abundant in the deserts of North America. The cactus produces fruits that you can find in the produce section of your supermarket. These prickly pears come in different varieties: yellow, purple, and white. Not only are the fruits edible and sweet, they have long been a sta-

18 ft

ple food of Native Americans. Here's a recipe for prickly pear jelly that uses only the juice from a prickly pear cactus.

What You Need

- *A grown-up to assist*
- 4 cups (.9 l) prickly pear juice
- 5 cups (1.2 l) sugar
- 1 tablespoon (14.8 ml) lemon juice
- Medium saucepan
- 2 packages of powdered pectin
- Wooden spoon
- 4 8-ounce (236-ml) jelly jars, thoroughly cleaned and dried

What You Do

1. Combine the prickly pear juice, sugar, and lemon juice in the saucepan and ask a grown-up to bring it to a boil.

2. Add the pectin and bring again to a boil. Do not let the liquid boil over. Boiling will cause the jelly to become stiffer.

3. Remove the mixture from the heat and skim off any foam from the top with the spoon.

4. Pour the liquid into the jelly jars, and seal according to the directions on the pectin package. Refrigerate. When the jelly is cool it can be added to cream cheese and spread on crackers for a yummy snack, or enjoyed on toast.

The Gila River

The Gila River (pronounced HEE-la) is the last waterway in New Mexico that is free of major dams and development. It begins in the spruce and pine forests of southwestern New Mexico's Gila Wilderness. It flows through a series of canyons before it enters the high-walled canyon called the Gila Middle Box and then continues on through

Arizona's Sonoran Desert and another steep-walled canyon. The river water is used for irrigation farther downriver and the water that remains ends up at the Colorado River.

The Gila River ecosystem is now threatened by a water withdrawal project. The plan would remove 18,000 acre-feet from the river every year, which is the amount of water necessary to cover over 28 square miles (72.5 sq km) to a depth of one foot (.3 m). Even though the plan is already being carried out, there is no use identified yet for the water removed.

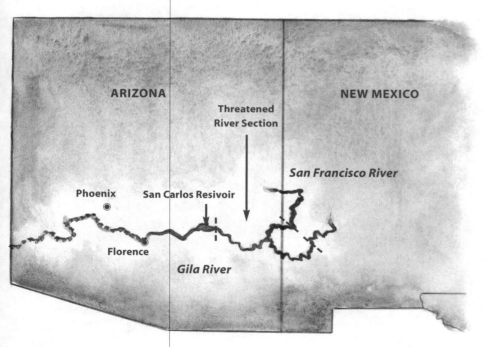

ARIZONA   NEW MEXICO

Threatened River Section

San Francisco River

Phoenix   San Carlos Resivoir

Florence

Gila River

Make a Rain Gauge

The more water you collect from rainfall, the less water you'll need to use from your faucet. This not only helps with conserving water resources, it will also help your water bill decrease. Years ago people collected water in barrels or tanks called cisterns. You can use buckets or barrels to collect water during rainstorms to water your lawn or garden. How much water do you think falls during an average rain shower? Could it be enough to water your entire lawn and garden? How long do you think it would take to fill a barrel? Make a rain gauge to measure the amount of rain that falls during a rain shower or rainstorm.

What You Need
- Clear glass jar (mayonnaise jars work well)
- Ruler

What You Do
1. Place the jar outside in an open area before it begins to rain.
2. Carry your jar inside after the rain stops falling.
3. Place your ruler against the side of the jar and see how many inches fell during the storm.

Imagine how much water you could collect to water your garden if this jar was the size of a barrel or a bathtub. Talk to your parents about creating a rain-catching device to help keep your lawn and garden watered when it's not raining.

The People of the Gila River

An Act of Congress established the Gila River Indian Lands in February 1859. The United States Constitution formed the Gila River Indian Community (GRIC) in central Arizona in 1939. The Community is an alliance of two Native American tribes, the Akimel O'odham and the Pee Posh. The community seal, depicting a cactus, mountains, and the river, symbolizes how the river brings life to the desert.

The ancestors of these people, the HuHuKam, developed extensive irrigation systems by digging canals from the Gila River into their fields. They grew maize, squash, beans, cotton, and tobacco. They also gathered fruits from the desert, such as prickly pears. The Akimel O'odham continued the practice of the HuHuKam and have irrigated thousands of acres of desert to plant and harvest.

Today the community harvests food from close to 15,000 acres (6,070 hectares) of land in the river basin in an enterprise called Gila River Farms.

River Rapids

Here's what you can do to help protect the Gila River. With the help of a grown-up, contact Senators Jeff Bingaman (D-NM), John McCain (R-AZ), and New Mexico Governor Bill Richardson to ask them to oppose any withdrawals of water from the Gila River in connection with the Arizona Water Settlements Act (S437). Contact information can be found in the Resource section.

Make a Community Seal

The Gila River Community seal depicts their dependence on the Gila River and the land where they live. Try your hand at creating a seal for your community.

What You Need

- Markers
- Paper

What You Do

1. What is important to your community? Think about landmarks that represent the area where you live, such as a clock tower that appears on town signs or other symbols. Write down your ideas.

2. Draw a large circle (about the size of the bottom of a bowl) to create the form for your seal. Draw a picture of what is important to your community in the circle.

3. Take a look at some other seals. Visit your town hall and see if there is a seal displayed there. Does your state have a seal? Your school? Your town? Compare your seal with these seals. Any similarities? Find out what the symbols in those seals represent.

The Trinity River

The Trinity River has three major branches: the East Fork, the Elm Fork, and the West Fork. In 1850, it was reported by army engineers that the river was the deepest and least obstructed river in Texas. Seven steamboats sailed the lower channel in the peak season of 1868, but with the advent of railroad travel to Dallas in the 1870s, river traffic slowed.

The waters of the Trinity became very polluted during the next century. Runoff carrying pesticides and herbicides (plant-killing chemicals) ran into the river, along with industrial and human waste. By the 1960s the river was so polluted that the United States Public Health Service described it as being septic, another word for infected. A water quality plan was developed in the 1970s to clean up

River:	**Trinity**
Length:	**500 miles (805 km)**
Cities Served by River:	**Dallas, Ft. Worth, Houston**
Riverkeeper:	**No**

the river, but the problems persisted. The Trinity River Authority is now in place and is working hard to clean the river. Fortunately progress has been made. There is a fishery that appears to be returning to a more or less normal state. To find out more about the Trinity River and the issues it faces check out the Trinity River Authority Web site at www.trinityra.org.

Let's Continue Our Journey

Wow, are you thinking of America as rivers yet? By now you've probably realized that these rivers flow in and out of regions in North America. The Gila River reaches the Colorado River and the Rio Grande flows all the way to Mexico. Our next stop brings us to the land of alligators, Mark Twain, steamboats, and alien mussels. Hey, we're going to explore some of the Midwest Rivers, including the granddaddy of them all—the Mississippi River! You'll see that these rivers also flow to other regions of North America. In fact, take a look at a map and find the Mississippi River and you'll see that it is a hard river to place in any one region because it's so long. OK, we're off.

Life *on* the Mississippi, Missouri, *and* Other Midwest Rivers

5

"The face of the water, in time, became a wonderful book—a book that . . . told its mind to me without reserve, delivering its most cherished secrets as if it uttered them with a voice. And it was not a book to be read once and thrown aside, for it had a new story to tell every day."

—Mark Twain, from *Life on the Mississippi*

Today, 12 million people call the areas that border the Mississippi River home, but a resident from the past comes to mind first when we think of that river: Mark Twain. His books, written over a century ago, brought the Mississippi to life. He was born Samuel Clemens in Florida, Missouri, in 1835, but moved with his family to Hannibal, on the shores of the Mississippi, when he was just four years old. This is where he drew inspiration for some of his greatest works, including the *Adventures of Huckleberry Finn* and *Life on the Mississippi*. So let's start this investigation of these Midwestern rivers with the man himself, Mark Twain, and then we'll take a look at some of the region's other history and its wildlife.

The Days of Mark Twain

Hannibal, Missouri, was a great place for a boy to grow up, and if Mark Twain, or little Sam Clemens, could tell you, he would share stories of days fishing, hunting for lost treasure, and swimming. How do you think the river looked to him back then? When Sam Clemens was a boy he saw steamboats and log rafts sailing down the river all the time. In fact, those steamboats were so exciting to him that as a young boy he dreamed of being a riverboat pilot when he grew up.

His dream came true in 1857, when at the age of 22 he was hired by the captain of the *Paul Jones* to be an apprentice, or cub, pilot. It was a great chance for him to learn even more about the Mississippi. He was taught the location of every sandbar, island, and submerged tree in the river. He also studied the changing water depths and the weather patterns. He finally became a pilot, but lucky for us his riverboat career ended when the Civil War broke out, and we now have the wonderful legacy of his stories. As we know, his knowl-

River:	Mississippi River and the Missouri River
Length:	3,895 miles (6,268 km)
Distinction:	Longest southward-flowing river
Major Tributaries:	Tennessee, Ohio, Platte, Cumberland, Red, Arkansas, Canadian
Cities Served by River:	New Orleans, Baton Rouge, Memphis, St. Louis, St. Paul, Minneapolis, Kansas City, Omaha, Great Falls, Billings, Denver, Louisville, Cincinnati, Pittsburgh, Nashville, Chattanooga, Knoxville, Little Rock, Oklahoma City, Tulsa, Wichita, Shreveport
American Heritage Designated Rivers:	Yes
Riverkeeper:	Yes
Watershed:	Mississippi: 1,245,000 square miles (3,225,000 sq km) (this includes Missouri)

River Rapids

Samuel Clemens didn't invent the name Mark Twain. It was a Mississippi riverboat term used to describe the depth of two fathoms, or 12 feet, in the river. The leadsman on the boat would yell out, "By the mark, twain!" Samuel Clemens first used the pseudonym Mark Twain on a travel article in 1863.

edge of the river and its people did not go to waste. He later used the town of Hannibal as the setting in *The Adventures of Tom Sawyer*. His memories of the river and the people who lived along it also impacted *Life on the Mississippi, A Tramp Abroad,* and many other works.

Huckleberry Finn Log Raft

Do you think you could build a log raft like Huck Finn? Follow these steps for one you can sail in your own bathtub.

What You Need

- *A grown-up to assist*
- 18 twigs, roughly 6 inches (15 cm) long
- Wood glue
- Sheet of paper
- Scissors
- Markers

What You Do

1. Place 12 of the twigs together side by side. Stand one stick up in the middle to form a mast between the sixth and seventh twigs.

2. Glue a twig crosswise along each end of the 12 sticks and on both sides of the mast to hold it in place.

3. Cut a triangle out of the sheet of paper to form your sail. Decorate it with markers and glue it to the mast.

4. Let the glue dry on your raft, then take it to a sink or bathtub. Does it float? Try sailing it in a small stream or puddle outside. Can you imagine sailing down a river on a raft?

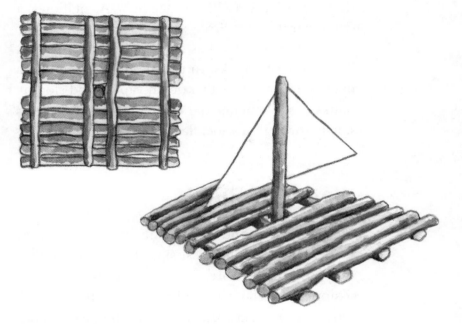

Old Man River

Thousands of years ago, during the Ice Age, the Mississippi River actually flowed north and emptied into a big lake. As the earth began to warm, the glaciers began to melt, leaving behind the rocks and soil they carried. This material dammed up old river valleys and formed the Great Lakes. Rivers were forced to make new routes to the ocean. The Mississippi then began its journey southward from its source at Lake Itasca in Minnesota. The river now flows through nine states on the way to the Gulf of Mexico. As it flows it demonstrates the three stages of a river. At the source it is described as a young river with a fast flow and steep banks. In the middle it resembles a mature river with worn down rapids and sloping banks. As it reaches the Gulf of Mexico it flows slowly through a wide, flat valley like an old river.

Wetlands Rule!

Melting snows and heavy rains often send a lot more water into the Mississippi River each spring. All of this extra water sometimes causes the Mississippi to overflow its banks. This is called a flood. Floodwater makes the soil near the river richer because it adds the nutrients from the river, but it can also cause damage. The waters can fill roads and threaten buildings that are built in the area. It can also wash away crops and damage farmland. Dams on the Ohio and Missouri Rivers help control the amount of water that flows into the Mississippi, but still floods occur.

Wetland areas along the river provide a buffer and help control the damage floods may cause. These wetlands act like sponges. They catch and hold the extra water to prevent flooding from occurring. During dry times, they help prevent brooks and streams from drying up and fish and other wildlife from dying by slowly releasing water. In addition, wetlands are important ecosystems that provide a habitat for many plants and animals, such as herons, muskrats, red-winged blackbirds, turtles, and ducks.

Many of these wetlands are being filled in and developed, which is destroying the buffer. See how wetlands work with this quick experiment.

What You Need
- Clear glass baking pan
- Florist's foam (as wide as the pan and several inches taller)
- Soil to fill half the pan
- Measuring cup
- Water

What You Do
1. Squeeze the foam and stand it up in the middle of the pan so that it divides the pan in half.
2. Add soil behind the foam on one side of the pan to fill it about halfway to the top of the pan.
3. The soil represents the land and the foam represents the wetland. Leave the other side of the pan empty.

4. Fill the measuring cup up with water and pour it into the soil. Keep adding the water.

5. What happens? Is the foam stopping the water? Press down on the foam and see how much water the foam absorbs.

6. Remove the foam. This is what it would be like if the wetlands were destroyed and didn't provide a buffer for the river. What happens? What does this mean to buildings close to the shore?

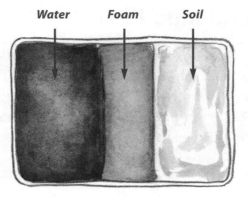

Water   Foam   Soil

Have you ever tried to hold back a wave?

It is almost impossible. Imagine waves that are as high as your school building. We cannot always protect our neighborhoods from the waves and water that develop from weather systems, but that doesn't mean we don't keep trying. *Levees* are natural or manmade embankments or dikes that run parallel to a river to help prevent flooding of the land alongside the river. They are usually built with dirt, but sandbags are sometimes used to enforce them. The levees of the Mississippi River comprise one of the largest levee systems of the world, making up 3,500 miles (5,600 km) of levees extending roughly 1,000 miles (1,600 km) alongside the Mississippi. They were established to protect the city of New Orleans from flooding. Other levees to protect New Orleans from the waters of nearby Lake Pontchartrain were also built. These levees failed during Hurricane Katrina in August 2005 when the storm surge created one of the worst natural disasters in U.S. history, and caused the complete evacuation of New Orleans, and was responsible for more than 1,000 deaths.

You can find out more about levees at www.mvm.usace.army.mil/floodcontrol/Levees/levees.htm or http://boe.cabe.k12.wv.us/habitat/levees.html.

Mississippi Mud Pie

The banks of the Mississippi are not always wet and flooded. Sometimes they are very dry and cracked. Make this Mississippi Mud Pie and see what the banks look like on dry days. It's a yummy alternative to the mud pies you might make after it rains.

What You Need

- *A grown-up to assist*
- 2 sticks butter
- ½ cup (118 ml) cocoa
- Saucepan
- Wooden spoon
- Mixing bowl
- 2 cups (473 ml) sugar
- 4 eggs, slightly beaten
- 1½ cups (355 ml) flour
- 1½ cups (355 ml) chopped pecans
- 1 teaspoon (5 ml) vanilla
- Pie tin, greased

What You Do

1. Place the butter and cocoa in the saucepan. Ask a grown-up to stir the mixture over a low heat until the butter melts.
2. Remove from the heat and pour into a mixing bowl. Add the sugar and eggs. Mix well.
3. Add the flour, nuts, and vanilla. Blend it well with the wooden spoon.
4. Pour into the greased pie tin. Bake at 360°F (36°C) for 35 to 40 minutes. Does your finished pie look like the dried banks of the Mississippi? It might, but it certainly tastes a whole lot better!

River Rapids

The Mississippi River dumps about 770 million short tons (698,532,250 metric tons) of mud and sand each year into the Gulf of Mexico. The *delta,* or fan-shaped area of land at the mouth of the river, that this sediment forms stretches about 200 miles (322 kilometers) into the gulf and is still growing.

The Mississippi Flyway

The Mississippi has not only served as a major waterway for human travel—millions of birds fly along the river and its tributaries during the spring and fall migration periods. In fact, 40 percent of North American waterfowl use the river as a *flyway,* or migratory path. Some birds, such as ducks and pelicans, use the open-water areas of the river as they migrate. Other birds, such as songbirds, geese, and egrets, use the more shallow backwater wetlands of the river. The river provides resting places and a food source for the birds as they travel the long distance to their destination.

Mississippi Flyway Bird Spotting

There are about 325 species of birds that use the flyway. Here are a few to look for:

- Wood duck
- Mallard duck
- Osprey
- American White Pelican
- Double-crested Cormorant
- Canada goose
- Black tern
- Great Blue Heron
- Snowy Egret

- Common Merganser
- American Bittern
- American Goldfinch
- Yellow-breasted Chat
- Yellow Warbler
- Scarlet Tanager
- American Robin
- Eastern Bluebird

Snowy Egret

Scarlet Tanager

Flyway Passport

Whether or not you live in the Mississippi flyway, you can track migratory birds in your area. Make this simple passport to help track your local birds on their migration.

What You Need

- *A grown-up to assist*
- 5 sheets 8½ by 11 inch unlined paper
- Crayons, colored pencils, or markers
- Ruler
- Pen or pencil
- Hole punch
- 3 pieces of yarn about 4 inches (10 cm) long
- Scissors
- Bird guidebook
- Binoculars

What You Do

1. Fold your paper in half so the sheets become 5½ by 8½ inches in size. Put them together to form a book of 10 pages with one page inside the other.

2. Decorate the cover of your Flyway Passport.

3. On the first four inside pages, make three columns using the ruler and pen or pencil. On the top of each page write BIRDS I HAVE SEEN. Label each column with DATE, PLACE, TYPE OF BIRD. Leave the remaining pages blank.

4. Use the hole punch to make three holes on the folded side of the passport book just inside the fold. Tie a piece of yarn through each hole and tie it in a bow.

5. Use your passport book during the spring and fall months to track the birds flying through your area during their migration. Use the bird guide and binoculars to identify the different species of birds you see. Record the information from your sightings in your passport. Draw pictures of the birds you see, take notes, or add photos of your discoveries to the blank pages of your passport.

Lower Mississippi Riverkeeper Mary Lee Orr

Mary Lee Orr didn't always want to be a riverkeeper; before she became one, she worked as a teacher and owned an art gallery. Orr says that a riverkeeper brings whatever skills he or she has to help preserve the river and combines that with a deep passion for protecting rivers. The Mississippi River is the magical, mystical river of Mark Twain novels, and Orr wants to remind readers that the river is a mirror that reflects what happens to us. As we pollute the rivers, we are polluting our own way of life.

Find out more about the Mississippi River and how you can help the Louisiana Action Network with the issues facing the region at www.leanweb.org.

Attack of the Killer Zebra Mussels

Native Mississippi mussels are facing suffocation by alien zebra mussels that attach themselves to the shells of the native species. The pink heelsplitter, wabash pigtoe, and fat mussels are three of the native mussels that are battling against the zebras.

Zebra mussels (*Dreissena polymorpha*) are native to the Caspian and Black Sea region. They are a small barnacle-type, freshwater mollusk. They were first spotted in North America in 1988 in Lake St. Clair, of the Great Lakes region of the United States, and have spread throughout many waterways, including the Mississippi, Ohio, Tennessee, Illinois, Arkansas, and Cumberland rivers. Scientists believe that the commercial ships that come into the lakes from across the sea released the mussels into the lake when they emptied their ballast water.

Ballast water is water that ships carry to become heavier, so they are more stable for the journey through large bodies of water. When the ship arrives at its destination, the ballast water is released into the port from the ship. Unfortunately, sediment, which also might include plants and animals, is often discharged into the port.

The mussels have caused many problems. They multiply quickly and compete with native mussels. They also feed by filtering plankton out of the water. The plankton is important to the river's food web. It provides food for other organisms and hiding places for young fish. When it disappears the water clarity changes and the animals that depend on the plankton suffer.

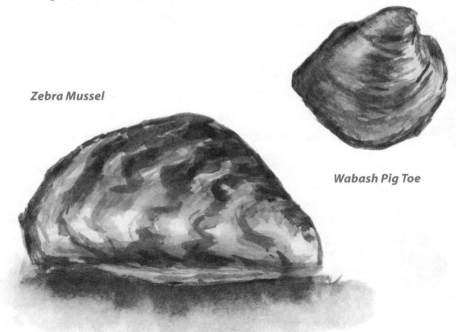

Zebra Mussel

Wabash Pig Toe

The Fight Back!

Scientists are trying to find a way to rid the rivers of these mussels. They found that chlorine kills them, but also harms other river life. They also found that water temperatures above 110°F (43°C) will kill the mussels and other river wildlife.

While scientists work to find out how to rid the rivers of the mussels, there are steps that we can take to help.

● When transporting a boat, make sure to drain out all the bilge water, the live wells, and the bait buckets before leaving areas that are infected with zebra mussels.

● Inspect the hull of the boat and all other areas that are exposed to infested waters. "Hitchhiking" mussels might make the hull feel grainy. If it does feel grainy with tiny mussels, ask a grown-up to scrape it clean with a paint scraper.

● Use water 140°F (60°C) or hotter to flush the hull and other areas that are exposed to river water.

● Make sure the boat and trailer are completely dry before they are used in another river.

Examine a Mussel

Freshwater mussels, including zebra mussels, are mollusks. They are bivalves, meaning they have a hinge and two shells. Buy some at your local grocery store at the seafood counter and take a closer look.

What You Need
● *A grown-up to assist*
● A mussel
● Cutting board or other flat surface
● Ruler

What You Do
1. Ask the person behind the seafood counter what type of mussel you are buying.
2. When you get home, use your ruler to measure your mussel. How long is it? Zebra mussels are usually about the size of an average adult fingernail. They can grow up to roughly 2 inches (50 mm). Is the mussel you are examining larger?

River Challenge
How would you control the zebra mussel population? Investigate what is being done now. Can you add any suggestions?

3. Find the hinge on your mussel. Is the mussel easy to open?

4. Ask a grown-up to open up your mussel for you. Examine the inside of the mussel. Does the shell look the same on the inside as it does on the outside? The smooth inner shell surface is called the *nacre*.

EXTERNAL SHELL

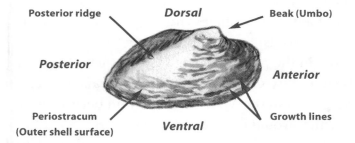

Posterior ridge · *Dorsal* · Beak (Umbo)

Posterior

Anterior

Periostracum (Outer shell surface) · *Ventral* · Growth lines

INTERNAL SHELL

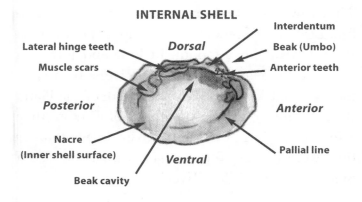

Interdentum

Lateral hinge teeth · *Dorsal* · Beak (Umbo)

Muscle scars · Anterior teeth

Posterior · *Anterior*

Nacre (Inner shell surface) · Pallial line

Ventral

Beak cavity

River Rapids

The *Continental Divide* is as much about rivers as it is about mountains. It is an imaginary line that runs along the *crest*, or highest point, of the Rocky Mountains, dividing both the United States and Canada. It also separates the waters that eventually flow into the Pacific Ocean from the waters that flow into the Atlantic Ocean. Streams run down the mountains and fall on one side or the other. On the west side they flow into waters that will eventually flow to the Pacific and on the east they flow into waters that will flow into the Atlantic. Look for the streams on a map. Those on the west side of the crest send their waters into the Snake, Columbia, and Colorado rivers. Streams that are east of the mountain crest flow into the Mississippi River by way of the Missouri, Arkansas, and Red rivers.

River of Song

Rivers connect people. They can also connect culture. There is no better way to see this than to check out the Smithsonian Institution's *River of Song* project. In 1997 the Smithsonian sent a production team up and down the Mississippi River. They spent 12 weeks and traveled 12,000 miles (19,312 km) researching and gathering film footage of musical acts that ranged from Minneapolis rock to St. Louis gospel and Memphis soul; from bluegrass bands in the Farm Belt to the blues in the Mississippi Delta; from Scandinavian fiddlers in the North Woods to Cajun stompers in the Louisiana bayous. Despite their differences, they were all inspired by their proximity to the mighty Mississippi. Their music flows together, overlaps, and comes out with unique American sounds. For more information on this project take a look at www.pbs.org/riverofsong/music/. Does your region have its own distinct music? How do your local rivers inspire the musicians in your region?

Stepping Back into History

It's time to take a look at the other rivers in this region, but before we do, we have to step back into the past and talk about Lewis and Clark. In 1803 President Thomas Jefferson asked Congress to approve $2,500 for an expedition to explore the West in order to search out a land route to the Pacific Ocean, which would strengthen American claims to Oregon territory. The expedition was also designed to gather information about the Native American inhabitants and the terrain of the

Far West. Congress agreed. Meriwether Lewis was to lead the expedition. He asked William Clark, an old friend from his army days, to join him. Clark designed a 55-foot (17-m) long keelboat for the journey. It was a boat that could be rowed, sailed, or pushed by poles. While he was waiting for the boat to be built in Pittsburgh, he purchased a Newfoundland dog to take with them on the journey. He named the dog Seaman.

The party of 31 men brought many items, including shiny bracelets, medals, mirrors, hats, and flags, to exchange with the Native Americans for materials and food. They set out on May 14, 1804, in the pouring rain. They pushed their keelboat and two flat-bottomed dugout canoes, called *pirogues,* into the Missouri River and began a journey that would open up the West.

Many days Lewis and Seaman walked along the riverbank while Clark steered the keelboat. They saw many beavers, passenger pigeons, and fish. Lewis and Clark journeyed along the Missouri River for roughly a month. In June and July they explored the Kansas and Platte Rivers. In August they were back on the Missouri, north of the Platte River. Before reaching the plains of Dakota they also explored the Big Sioux River. In September they were on the Teton River, which the Teton Sioux called the "Bad River."

Winter arrived and the men camped at Fort Mandan. Lewis and Clark hired a French Canadian trapper to accompany them as an interpreter. His wife, Sacagawea, a Shoshone, proved to be even more useful than her husband. Her presence with the party helped smooth relations with other Native Americans they met on the rest of their journey.

By April the party was back on the Missouri River. In August of that year the party reached the source of the Missouri, but the expedition didn't end there. Lewis and Clark were determined to reach the Pacific Ocean. They continued on horseback until they reached the Columbia River. It was October 1805. After sailing the rapids on the river, the party finally reached the Pacific Ocean on November 7, 1805.

Lewis and Clark Trail

LOUISIANA PURCHASE

Lucky Lewis and Clark Journal

Lewis encountered many plants and animals on the expedition west. He recorded them in his journal and collected specimens to bring back to Pennsylvania. He buried many of the specimens he collected, including bird feathers, animal skins, and plants, in packages, planning to uncover them on the return trip, but when he did uncover them, most were damaged by flood waters. Lewis lost many of his specimens, and his journal washed over the boat on the Missouri River. Sacajawea scooped as many pages as she could out of the water, but he lost most of it. It must have been heartbreaking for him.

River Rapids

When Lewis and Clark embarked on their expedition, there were still many unexplored places in the world. Times have changed and not many unexplored places are left. If you could explore a part of our world, where would you go? If you lived at the time of Lewis and Clark, where would you have explored then?

Follow in Lewis's footsteps to create your own journal. With better luck you'll have yours for years to come. Here's how.

What You Need

- *A grown-up to assist*
- Cardboard
- Pencil
- Ruler
- Scissors
- Decorative paper for cover
- White craft glue
- Paintbrush
- White paper
- Paper hole puncher
- 2½-inch (6.4-cm) notebook rings

What You Do

1. Measure and cut two 6-by-6-inch (15.2-cm) squares of cardboard for the covers of your book.

2. Measure and cut two 7-by-7-inch (17.7-cm) squares of decorative paper. You can use tissue paper, handmade paper, wrapping paper, or wallpaper to decorate the covers of your book.

3. Place the decorated side of your paper facing down on a flat surface. Place the cardboard centered on top of the decorative sheet. Use the scissors to make a tiny slit in each corner of the decorative paper. Do not cut the cardboard.

4. Lift the cardboard back up and using the paintbrush, spread each decorative sheet with white glue. Place the cardboard back in position on top of the decorative sheet.

5. Use the paintbrush to apply a line of glue on the edges of the cardboard. Then fold up the edges of the decorative paper. Let the covers dry.

6. Measure and cut several 6-by-6-inch sheets of paper for the inside pages of your journal.

7. Line up the pages inside the two covers and ask a grown-up to help punch two holes in your book roughly ¼ inch (1.3 cm) from one side.

8. Place a ring in each hole. Now your book is ready for you to record your discoveries. Bring along a pencil to record your findings and some colored pencils for your sketches. The rings will allow you to add more pages as you fill the book up.

Time to Shoot the Hooch!

We're moving to the southeast. We'll "shoot the hooch," discover the Chesapeake Bay, and ride a paddleboat on the Tennessee. Turn the page for more discoveries.

"Shoot the Hooch" and Other Fun on Southeastern Rivers

6

"So—this—is—a—River!"
"THE River," corrected the Rat.
"And you really live by the river?
  What a Jolly life!"

—Kenneth Grahame, from
  The Wind in the Willows

The riverside picnic in Kenneth Grahame's book *The Wind in the Willows* wasn't set beside a southeastern United States river, but it might have been. Grahame saw the same relationships between wildlife and rivers in Scotland as we see here. Rivers mean so much to their wildlife, and to us. As we have seen in other chapters, we rely on rivers for transportation, energy, water, recreation, and many other things. Sometimes it's wonderful to just sit beside a river and ponder its existence, soak up its energy, and enjoy its grandeur. The rivers of the southeast are just perfect for some of those lazy days.

Bottled Sunshine Punch

Sit beside a free flowing river with a picnic lunch. Take a copy of *The Wind in the Willows* and read about Ratty's picnic. Then, just like Ratty, spread out a blanket and share some yummy treats. Ratty brought along some French bread, a sausage, some cheese, and a flask containing bottled sunshine. Here's a quick recipe for your own Bottled Sunshine Punch to bring along.

River Otter

What You Need

- *A grown-up to assist*
- ¼ cup (118 ml) sugar
- ½ cup (118 ml) water
- Saucepan
- Wooden spoon
- Pitcher
- 2 cups (473 ml) apple juice
- ½ cup (118 ml) lemon juice
- Ice
- Thermos

What You Do

1. Combine the sugar and water in a saucepan and ask a grown-up to heat it over medium heat until the sugar dissolves.

2. Pour the mixture into a pitcher and add the apple juice and lemon juice. Refrigerate.

3. When you are ready for your picnic, pour the punch into a thermos and add some ice.

The Otter

Did you see any animals during your riverside picnic? It is difficult to hide a smile when watching an otter run up a river bank, then slide playfully down into the water on its belly. Once in the water, the otter makes graceful rolls and somersaults. Otters certainly look like they enjoy life!

Historically, otters were found widely throughout North America, but like the beaver, early trappers and fur traders hunted the otter. The otter's dense, durable fur helped Native Americans keep warm during winter and was also popular as trim on the coats of rich Europeans.

Otters are well adapted to their life in the water, being equipped with rudderlike tails, valved ears and nostrils to keep out water, and streamlined bodies. Like a flexible tornado, the otter swims rapidly through water with both speed and accuracy.

They use their long whiskers to nose along muddy river bottoms for crayfish, frogs, and salamanders. They will also raid bird, rabbit, and turtle nests on shore and have even been known to puncture a beaver dam and collect frogs and fish left stranded by the receding water.

You might spot a worn-down area on the shoreline of a river where the otters have pulled themselves out of the water. These are called *haul-outs*. Check them out, but be careful not to disturb them.

Be a Detective

Look around the river's shoreline. What animals do you think visited the water for a drink or to fish? Do you see any signs that they were there before you? Here's your chance to be a detective and find out what animals visited the river recently.

What You Need

- File folder
- Scissors
- Magnifying glass
- Plaster of paris
- Water
- Coffee can with a plastic lid
- Paper clips
- Ruler
- Field guide

What You Do

1. Cut the file folder up into strips about 1½ inches (4 cm) wide.

2. Look at the ground carefully. Use your magnifying glass. Do you see any animal footprints? These footprints, or tracks, will tell us what animal was at the river. Was there more than one animal? Were they all the same species or were they different? Select the track that you will "cast" and pick out any loose dirt or leaves from it.

3. Take a strip of file folder and form a collar around the track. Press it into the dirt slightly so that the plaster won't seep out when it is poured in.

4. Mix the plaster of paris and water in the can. Stir the mixture with a stick until it resembles pancake batter. Add more water or more plaster until it reaches this consistency.

5. Pour the plaster into the collar around the track. Make sure the plaster fills the collar and track.

6. Before the plaster hardens, pull apart the paper clip slightly and embed one side into the plaster, letting the other end act as the hook so that you will be able to hang your plaster cast. Press it into the plaster.

7. After the plaster is completely dry and hard—anywhere from ½ hour to three hours depending on weather conditions—carefully remove the collar and lift the cast up.

8. Brush off any loose dirt from your cast. Now it's time to identify your track. What animal do you think made that track? Take a look at a field guide of tracks and see what animal track matches your cast. Use the ruler to measure the length to help identify the track. What is the width of the print? Does the print indicate that the animal has claws? How do you know this? What else can you tell from this print? Is there any evidence in the area surrounding the print that gives you more information to help you identify the animal and determine its habits?

The James River

The James River was the first river to be named in the United States. The James is steeped in history—a history that includes many "firsts." It was the site of the first permanent English settlement in America, named Jamestown after the English King James I. It was here that Pocahontas, the Native American daughter of Chief Powhatan, lived with her English husband, John Rolfe, until they left for England in 1616. You may know of Pocahontas from other stories. She saved the life of

River: James

Length: 304 miles (489 km)

Distinction: Explored in 1607 by Captain John Smith

Cities Served by River: Richmond and Hampton, Virginia

Riverkeeper: Yes

Watershed: 10,000 square miles (25,900 sq km)

Captain John Smith and began a friendly relationship between the English and the Native Americans. The James River was also the home to the first colonial capital at Williamsburg. Over the centuries the James River region has been the site of conquests, revolutions, massacres, rebellions, and adventures.

The James River is the longest waterway contained in one state. It begins in the Allegheny Mountain foothills and meanders its way through the state of Virginia, providing food, energy, and a means of transportation before emptying into the Chesapeake Bay.

James Riverkeeper Chuck Fredrickson

Chuck Fredrickson is the riverkeeper for the James River and has worked to protect it for almost 45 years. His background as a teacher, administrator, and fisherman has helped him in his riverkeeping work. He gets upset when people show a disregard for the health of the river in favor of building without taking the ecology of the river into account. Sewer overflows from the city of Richmond threaten the water quality of the river. It's

important to protect the crucial habitats and riparian areas of the James River. Fredrickson urges us to protect its natural and historic resources for future generations. Kids can find out more about the issues facing the James River at the James River Association Web site at www.jamesriverassociation.org or www.jamesriverinfo.org.

The Chesapeake Bay

American Bald Eagle

We cannot discuss the rivers of North America without exploring the bay that over 150 rivers and streams drain into, including the Potomac, James, Susquehanna, Appomattox, and Patuxent. It is the largest bay in the United States and one of the shallowest, averaging only 21 feet (6 m) deep. Native Americans knew the Chesapeake Bay as "Chesepiooc" or "Great Shellfish Bay," named for its abundance of crabs, oysters, and clams. It yields

Blue Crab

River Challenge

Find out about river cleanup events in your region. Is there an annual event? Find out how to participate. The James River has had river cleanups in various locations on the river for many years. The James River Advisory Council was set up to help organize these cleanups over six years ago. Each year the James River Regional cleanup continues to grow with the help of canoeists, hikers, community members, business owners, environmental organizations, and local government. You can help with the cleanup by registering online at www.jamesriveradvisorycouncil.com/cleanup/cleanup.htm.

more fish and shellfish than any of the 130 other estuaries in the United States. But fish and shellfish are not the only wildlife that call the bay home; there are sea turtles, eagles, sharks, osprey, and shad among the other species in the bay.

River Rapids

There are 162 nonnative plant, animal, and *microbe* (microscopic organisms such as protozoa) species that have been released purposefully or accidentally by people over the last two centuries thriving in the Chesapeake Bay, according to the Smithsonian Environmental Research Center in Edgewater, Maryland. These aliens, like any predators, wreak havoc in the bay's ecosystem. The mute swan is an example of one of these species. Released in 1962, the mute swan drives off native waterfowl and devours aquatic plants in the bay. (See Chapter 5 for information about zebra mussels, which are another challenging predatory species that affects some rivers.)

Shad

The Potomac River

The Potomac River winds its way through the Appalachian Mountains, past historic battlefields, old towns, and the Washington, Jefferson, and Lincoln memorials in Washington, D.C. In fact, it is often called "the nation's river" because it flows right through the capital of the United States.

The Potomac Conservancy has formed River Restoration Action Teams, or River RATs, to commit their energy, skills, and other resources to help

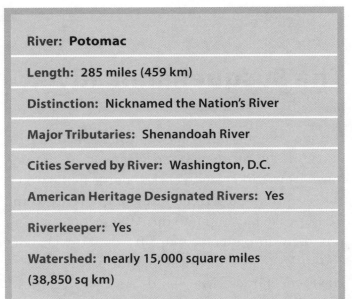

River: Potomac

Length: 285 miles (459 km)

Distinction: Nicknamed the Nation's River

Major Tributaries: Shenandoah River

Cities Served by River: Washington, D.C.

American Heritage Designated Rivers: Yes

Riverkeeper: Yes

Watershed: nearly 15,000 square miles (38,850 sq km)

protect this beautiful and historic river. The RATs take on specific projects, including trash cleanup and tree planting along the riverbanks. They also work to remove alien plant species, such as invader vines and shrubs, that have taken up residence on the banks of the river. These alien species choke out the native plants that are important members of the diverse river ecosystem.

If you know any grown-ups who would be interested in joining a River Restoration Action Team, tell them they can log on to www.potomac.org/action/riverrats/index.html and register for a project that interests them.

The Susquehanna River

It is amazing to think that you can stand at a tributary of the Susquehanna River near Cooperstown, New York, place a corked bottle in the water, and eventually it will float down the river to the Chesapeake Bay and into the Atlantic Ocean. Can you follow its path on a map? It would travel about 400 miles (644 km) to the mouth of the river at Havre de Grace, Maryland. As the river flows through the mid-Atlantic states of Pennsylvania and Maryland, it is called "the mighty Susquehanna" because it is the largest river entirely in the United States that drains into the Atlantic Ocean. It is about a mile (1.6 km) wide near Harrisburg, Pennsylvania.

Audubon Pennsylvania has developed a wonderful guide for birding and wildlife watching along the Susquehanna River. You can find out how to order it at www.pabirdingtrails.org.

River: Susquehanna

Length: 450 miles (724 km)

Distinction: Drowned lower valley became Chesapeake Bay

Cities Served by River: Harrisburg, Wilkes-Barre, Binghampton

American Heritage Designated Rivers: Yes

Riverkeeper: No

Brackish Water Experiment

River water that flows into the ocean is freshwater. There might be some water near the ocean that is considered *brackish*, meaning it is a mixture of the salt water and freshwater, but overall the river water has much less salt content than the ocean water. What do you think happens to the river water when it flows into the ocean? Try this experiment to see for yourself.

What You Need

- 4 clear plastic cups
- Masking tape
- Marker
- Measuring cup
- Water
- Sea salt
- Measuring spoon
- Food coloring
- Eyedropper

What You Do

1. Using the masking tape and marker, label each cup A, B, C, or D. Pour one cup of water into the cups marked A and B.

2. Add 1 tablespoon (15 ml) of salt into cups A and B. Stir the solution until the salt dissolves. Add 2 additional teaspoons (10 ml) of salt into cup A to make an extra-salty solution.

3. Pour about ¼ cup (59 ml) of the salt solution from cup B into cup C. Add 5 drops of food coloring to the cup.

4. Pour about ¼ cup of the extra salty solution from cup A into cup D.

5. Using the eyedropper, drop about 15 drops of the colored solution into cup D. What happens when the less salty water is introduced to the extra salty solution? Does it float or sink? What do you think would happen if you did this experiment with the other solutions and dropped the extra salty solution into the less salty solution?

The Tennessee River

Once a free-flowing river, the Tennessee River now has nine dams to protect the people and businesses that have settled near it from flooding rains. The dams allow the water to be regulated so that water can be released more slowly. The dams provide electricity for businesses and residents and water in times of drought. The Tennessee Valley Authority, the nation's largest power provider, maintains and operates all of the dams. A series of locks are maintained and operated by the Army Corps of Engineers, the world's largest public engineering, design, and construction management agency, run by the United States Army. The Continental Congress formed the Corps in 1775 to build fortifications near Boston at Bunker Hill. Their projects have continued throughout the country since those early days.

Look, It's Aunt Inga!

No, it's not really Aunt Inga; that large bird you might spy in the wetlands near the river is called an anhinga. The name is actually derived from the South American name *anhinga* (a water turkey). It is also sometimes called the snake-bird because of its long neck.

The American anhinga lives near water that has plants, such as willows, that it can nest and roost in. It uses its pointed bill to feed on fish in freshwater or in the brackish water found in estuaries. It also eats small aquatic animals, such as frogs. The anhinga is listed as endangered in Kentucky and of "special concern" in Tennessee and North Carolina. The designation of "special concern" means that the population numbers have not dropped low enough to be declared threatened or endangered, but that the numbers have diminished

Anhinga

and it is important to keep watch on the species so that the numbers do not decline further.

Anhingas are easy to spot. You can often see them drying their wings on a tree branch. They spread their wings straight out as though they are about to take off into the air, but instead they sit and let the warm air and sunshine dry their feathers. From tip to tip their wingspan can be four feet wide (1 m). How tall are you? Measure yourself and compare your height to an anhinga's wingspan. Now stretch your arms as far as you can to either side. How does your armspan compare to this bird's wingspan?

The Chattahoochee River

The Chattahoochee (chat-tah-HOO-chee) River begins as a trickle out of a spring in the mountain pass known as the Chattahoochee Gap. This Georgian river supplies 70 percent of the city of Atlanta's drinking water, which adds up to about 300 million gallons (1 billion l) per day. Considered the most heavily used water resource in Georgia, the Chattahoochee also supplies water for irrigation, power, industry, transportation, and recre-

ation. Sound familiar? Like all rivers, the Chattahoochee is a major resource for the people living and working in its watershed.

River: Chattahoochee

Length: 508 miles (817.5 km)

Distinction: Southernmost habitat for trout in U.S.

Major Tributaries: Flint

Cities Served by River: Atlanta

Riverkeeper: Yes

Watershed: 8,770 square miles (22,714 sq km)

River Rapids
Chattahoochee is a Creek Native American word meaning "painted rocks."

Upper Chattahoochee Riverkeeper Sally Bethea and Chattahoochee Riverkeeper Jim Phillips

Sally Bethea and Jim Phillips are both Chattahoochee riverkeepers. More than three million people each day depend on this river for drinking water, but this river is very polluted from the impact of Atlanta's development. The river is being contaminated by storm runoff polluted with sediment from construction sites. The river is also challenged by overuse, which occurs when individuals and communities withdraw water for both water supply and industrial use.

Bethea grew up loving to play in the streams near her house. She always wanted to do something

to help the larger community, but she didn't know she would become a riverkeeper. In fact, Bethea didn't even know what a riverkeeper was until about 10 years ago. Her master's degree in city planning with an emphasis on environmental planning is a tool that helps her care for this river.

Phillips has a science background and his knowledge of biology comes in handy in his work as a riverkeeper. He thinks that having good information is very important when forming public policy. Phillips didn't always want to be a riverkeeper; he planned on being a fireman or a football player. But he changed his mind once he learned that our rivers are in jeopardy.

Kids can find out more about the challenges to the Chattahoochee River at the Web site for the Upper Chattahoochee Riverkeeper at www.chattahoochee.org and can help the Chattahoochee with the Adopt-A-Stream program sponsored by the riverkeeper organization.

The Golden Age of the Chattahoochee

The Civil War took its toll on the Chattahoochee River. Both the Union and Confederate sides saw the river as an important waterway to control. By the time the war ended the river was full of silt and boat wreckage. But as the people of the Chattahoochee recovered, so did the river. It would never become as central to commerce as it was before the war, but the golden age of steamboating was close at hand.

After the war the boats became more opulent and less utilitarian, or down-to-earth. The *Naiad* was the most well-known steamboat on the river, and its food service was renowned. Guests enjoyed plates brimming with shrimp, oysters, and other fresh fish. By 1900 the service on the river was beginning to slow down. Instead of stopping at

every homestead or business on the river, the steamboats stopped in only the major communities. The shallowness of the river during periods of low rainfall also slowed down the river traffic. Railroads and automobiles soon became the major modes of transportation in the region.

"Shoot the Hooch"

Locals like to "shoot the hooch" (go rafting) on the Chattahoochee. Each spring Georgia Tech students and other college students hold a rafting contest on the river. Decorative rafts and inner tubes coast down the Chattahoochee. The only rule is that the crafts can't be engine powered. Whatever you call it, "shooting the hooch" is a great way to spend an afternoon up close and personal with the Chattahoochee River.

Here's how to decorate a raft or inner tube. Even if you're in a wading pool in your backyard and nowhere near the Chattahoochee River, you can still float in style.

What You Need
- Raft or inner tube
- Stickers
- Plastic streamers
- Life preservers
- Duct tape

What You Do
1. Use stickers, plastic streamers, or other objects to decorate your raft or inner tube. Keep in mind that it will be in the water, so your decorations will get wet. Be sure to place them where they can be seen.

2. Dress your raft up to look like a steamboat, a bed, or something else fun. Have a contest with your friends and family. Who has the craziest tube? Prettiest? Most inventive?

3. Launch your rafts or tubes in a quiet, shallow part of the river or in your backyard wading pool. Have a great time with your family and friends slowly moving down the lazy river, or just close your eyes and pretend. Be sure to wear your bathing suit and a life preserver.

◉ **Note:** It is not safe to "shoot the hooch" after heavy rains when the river is very muddy, for health reasons. Check out the Resources section for Web sites to help you find information for the Chattahoochee.

Heading North

The rivers of the southeast meander through fields and forests providing homes for egrets, herons, turtles, alligators, catfish, and other wildlife. Their waters are warmer than rivers up north and often a bit muddier. If you visited this region what would you want to do on these rivers? Would you fish for catfish, go crabbing in the Chesapeake, "shoot the hooch," ride a riverboat, or picnic on a riverbank? Look at the Resource section for more places to visit and explore. Now it's time to head north to explore the rivers there. Ready? Let's go.

Rivers of the Northeast

7

"Friends of my heart, lovers of nature's works,

Let me transport you to those wild, blue mountains

That rear their summits near the Hudson's wave."

—Thomas Cole, from
The Wild

This chapter begins with a quote by Thomas Cole, the founder of the Hudson River School of Painting. Thomas Cole was just one of many artists inspired by the mighty Hudson River in New York State, the first river we'll explore in this chapter. We'll also learn more about the Hudson River School of Art. Afterward, we'll move on to discover the Connecticut, Delaware, and the Kennebec rivers. These northeastern rivers were among the first traveled in the New World, even before our country was a country. The land was wild and the rivers ran free. Let's see what they've become.

The Hudson River

Ask any New Yorker to name a river and the first one that will come to mind is probably not the Nile or the Rhine . . . but the Hudson. This is understandable because the largest and most important river in New York State is the Hudson River.

If we search through the history of New York State, the importance of the Hudson River to its people, wildlife, and economic development becomes very clear.

River: **Hudson**	
Length: 315 miles (507 km)	
Distinction: One of the most important commerce highways in the United States	
Major Tributaries: Includes the Moodna and Fishkill Creeks	
Cities Served by River: New York, Albany, Utica	
American Heritage Designated Rivers: Yes	
Riverkeeper: Yes	
Watershed: 13,344 square miles (34,561 sq km)	

Hundreds of years before Henry Hudson sailed from Amsterdam in the Netherlands to what is now Albany, New York, the area was inhabited by Native Americans. According to a legend, the Native Americans came to the Hudson Valley searching for a river that flowed both ways. Their search was over when they found the *tidal* Hudson River. The flow of tidal rivers is affected by the same gravitational pull of the moon that causes the level of the ocean to rise and fall.

The richness of the river and its valley made living easier for the Algonquins, who controlled the Hudson. Striped bass, caught in the spring, were not only eaten fresh but were also smoked for later seasons. Deer were driven into the river and hunted to achieve a bountiful harvest. Food was not the only use of the river for the Algonquins. It was the primary route of travel, because it was much safer than ground travel. It also served as an important territorial boundary.

Hudson, an Englishman hired by the Moscovy Company to find a quick way from England to the spice islands of the Far East, reached Albany on September 1, 1609. Among the gifts that the Algonquins brought to Hudson on his ship, the *Halfmoon*, were beaver skins. As an item of trade, beaver skins played a major role in the development of New York for the next 200 years.

The abundant fur-bearing resources in the land Hudson called New Netherland stirred great interest in Holland. Dutch traders flocked to the Hudson Valley in search of furs. What is now known as Albany was in fact called "Beverwyck," or "Beaver Town," at this time. The river opened up trade routes north to Canada and west to the Great Lakes.

By 1671, around 80,000 beaver and otter skins gathered along New Netherland waterways were shipped to Europe. There, merchants routinely paid ten times the original price for the pelts and made them into coats and hats. Because of the abundance of navigable rivers for transport, Albany remained a dominant fur-trading center through the mid-1800s.

During the 1600s patroonships, or manors, were established in the valley. The requirements for these estates were that they be on the Hudson or another navigable river within the Dutch East India Company boundaries, which included the Mohawk River.

The English seized New Netherland in 1664, and changed the name of the area to New York and the name of the river to the Hudson. Beverwyck was renamed Albany. New York was still known to many as the Empire of the Beaver. Even today New York is known as the Empire State.

After the American Revolutionary War in the 1700s, the Hudson Valley became increasingly populated. Until the Mississippi Valley was settled more than a century later, the Hudson River was the most prominent and profitable waterway in America.

The population surrounding the Hudson River continued to grow. Railroads came to the valley in the 1800s. The river attracted industries and their workers up and down the valley. Agriculture flourished. In the 1900s power companies and

River Rapids

As a 13-year-old boy, Robert Fulton connected a paddlewheel to a fishing boat. Years later his creativity and imagination led him to put a steam engine in the hull of a ship, and he introduced steamboats to the world. In 1807, Robert Fulton introduced this new form of water navigation, piloting his *North River Steamboat,* later called the *Clermont,* on the Hudson River. The steamboats quickly became popular for recreational and commercial purposes. Steamboats, luxuriously furnished with pianos, bands, and dance rooms, sailed from Manhattan to Albany. It became more popular to sail to Albany than to Europe.

automobile manufacturers joined the growing list of industries on the river. Albany became a major port city.

The Hudson River has undergone many changes since the Algonquins put their canoes in the water, and the river has been challenged in many new ways, but its beauty and importance remain constant.

Hudson Riverkeeper Alex Matthiessen

Alex Matthiessen thinks the Hudson River is the richest river in the United States in terms of its ecology and its cultural and commercial history as a major waterway on the East Coast. It is also one of the most beautiful rivers in the world. Matthiessen was inspired to become a riverkeeper by his father, a writer and naturalist, who showed him from a young age the effects people can have on natural resources. Matthiessen was encouraged to give back something to make the world a better and safer place. Matthiessen has a degree in biology and environmental studies and a master's degree in public policy, and he points out that people working in the waterkeeper movement have all kinds of backgrounds, from commercial fishermen and boat captains to a Marine and professionally trained environmentalists.

Matthiessen is excited when he can see definite changes happening on the Hudson River, such as helping to promote technologies that reduce the number of fish killed by riverside power plants. Kids can learn more about this issue at: http://river keeper.org/campaign.php/fishkills. Kids can make a difference to their local river by reporting polluters to the riverkeeper near them.

Painting Nature

The Hudson River School was not an actual school building with art students. It was a group of painters who followed the same art style beginning in the middle of the nineteenth century. It was America's first landscape painting. The artists of the Hudson River School, such as Frederic Church, created works of art that showed the Hudson Valley wilderness. Many people thought the wilderness was dark, scary, and wild. These paintings encouraged people to explore the outdoors by showing how beautiful the wilderness was in the region. The Hudson River painters created their landscapes outside. They sometimes painted the same scene at different times of the day or year.

Here's your chance to create a work of art outdoors like the painters of the Hudson River School.

What You Need

- Blanket or chair to sit on outside
- Watercolor paper
- Watercolors
- Cup
- Water
- Paintbrushes
- White glue

What You Do

1. Pick a spot outside to create your piece of art. Set up your chair or blanket and sit for a while looking at your surroundings. What do you see? What does the sky look like? Is it bright blue or are there other colors in it? Think about what you want to paint.

2. Use your watercolors to paint a picture of what you see while you are sitting outside. Remember to rinse your brush in a cup of water between colors.

3. Wait two hours and return to your original spot. Notice the changes in the light and shadow as the sun moves across the sky. See how the area you originally painted has changed. Repaint this same area on another piece of paper and let your painting reflect the current colors that dominate this area. If you like, do this again in another two hours to record the further changes in color and shadow.

4. After you have completed your picture, let it dry. While it is drying, look around for leaves, feathers, and other bits of your surroundings to include in your picture.

5. When your picture is dry you can glue the objects on your picture. Keep in mind that heavy objects like stones might fall off. Show your picture to your friends and family and tell them about all the things you saw while you were creating it.

River Challenge

Visit the library or museum and look at paintings from Hudson River School painters such as Thomas Cole and Frederic Church. Also take a look at books by Thomas Locker, an artist who paints in the Hudson River style and has created many picture books for children.

Clean Water Congress

The Hudson Basin River Watch, a water conservation group based in East Greenwich, New York, sponsors the Clean Water Congress, a competitive event for schools and environmental groups located in the Hudson River watershed. It is held at the Darrow School in Columbia County, the Westchester Government Center in White Plains, and the Teatown Lake Reservation in Westchester County. Each winter and spring, teachers, students, and community participants monitor the physical, chemical, and biological characteristics of the Hudson River and its tributaries. The Congress looks at a number of factors that impact the watershed.

At the 2004 Congress, students had the chance to perform a "Mock Stream Analysis," in which they conducted water chemistry tests on a water specimen from a "mystery stream" and documented their results. From this data students then determined the health of the stream and offered possible explanations for their findings. All the teams that participated and met the objectives of this experiment were awarded certificates of achievement. The results were analyzed and presented at the Congress and to community and industry leaders, with the hope of increasing awareness of the river's issues and enabling groups to work together on solutions. For more information see the Hudson River Basin Web site at www.hudsonbasin.org/abouthbrw.html.

The Hudson's Mysterious Castle

If you ever take a ride on a Metro North train along the Hudson River and pass by the towns of Cold Spring and Garrison on the way to New York City, you might catch a glimpse out the window of a small island in the Hudson and a castle turret on

it. The island is named Pollepel Island and sits between Breakneck Ridge and Storm King Mountain. The castle ruins you see are the remains of the Bannerman Castle.

The island has a mysterious history. Long before Frank Bannerman purchased the island and built his castle, there were tales that the island was haunted. There is also a tale that a girl named Polly Pell was rescued from the breaking river ice, landed on the shore of the island, and promptly got married to her rescuer. We do know that the island was used against the British fleet during the American Revolution.

Frank Bannerman thought it was the ideal place for his military surplus store storage. He had been born in Scotland and he built his castle to resemble the Scottish castles of his homeland. Frank and his wife, Helen, spent summers on the island and planted many flowers and shrubs.

The island became the property of the Taconic Park Commission in 1967. Unfortunately a fire did a great deal of damage a few years later. Today the castle is a property of the New York State Office of Parks, Recreation, and Historic Preservation and has limited public access. There is still much work to be done to restore the property and make it safe for visitors. Find out how you can see the castle in the Resources section.

The Delaware River

Beginning in New York's Catskill Mountains, the Delaware River flows into two branches, the East Branch and the West Branch. The West Branch flows until it forms a boundary between Pennsylvania and New York. The East Branch runs parallel to the West Branch but eventually becomes the border between Pennsylvania and New Jersey. It continues on as the Lower Delaware River and

River: Delaware
Length: 315 miles (507 km)
Distinction: George Washington crossed the Delaware River in 1776
Major Tributaries: Schuylkill and Lehigh Rivers
Cities Served by River: Trenton, Philadelphia, Reading, Allentown, Wilmington, Easton
American Heritage Designated Rivers: No
Riverkeeper: Yes
Watershed: 13,539 square miles (35,066 sq km)

becomes the boundary for a few miles between New Jersey and the state of Delaware, where it eventually drains into Delaware Bay.

Perhaps the Delaware River is best known as the river George Washington crossed during the American Revolution. On the cold winter night of Christmas, 1776, Washington led his troops across the Delaware River. The very next day they defeated the British and German mercenaries in the Battle of Trenton.

The river is also known for the gorge it cut through the Kittatinny Mountains, creating the Delaware Water Gap. The gorge is about 2 miles (3 km) long. On the western side it is flanked by Mount Minsi in Pennsylvania, and on the opposite side by Mount Tammany in New Jersey. The cliffs are breathtaking and rise about 1,200 feet (365 m) above the water.

Oil Spill Newsflash!

On November 27, 2004, a tanker spilled 30,000 gallons (113,562 l) of oil on the Delaware River. Floating barriers contained the spill and skimmer vessels cleaned up, but the U.S. Fish and Wildlife Service reported that 50 birds had been killed and another 300 were in danger.

Oil spills are a danger on many of the rivers in North America. There are a few ways to clean oil from water, but none of them are perfect. First the spill is contained so that it does not spread into other areas. The oil floats on the top of the water, creating a layer. Then the oil can be skimmed off the surface. Or it can be soaked up or sunk to the bottom of the river.

Solve the Spill

Investigate the different ways that oil can be cleaned up from a river with this activity.

What You Need
- Water
- Large dish pan
- Cooking oil
- Drinking straws
- Sand
- Paper towel

What You Do

1. Pour the water into the dish pan. Fill it halfway. Pour enough oil to create a layer on top of the water. That's your oil spill.

2. Imagine you are on the task force to clean up this spill. What will you try to use first?

3. Experiment with the straw, sand, paper towel, or anything else you can think of to remove the oil. What works best? Can you imagine a spill that consists of over 30,000 gallons (113, 500 l) of oil?

The Connecticut River

New England's largest river ecosystem, the Connecticut River, flows through four New England states: Connecticut, Massachusetts, New Hampshire, and Vermont. It begins in an evergreen forest near Pittsburg, New Hampshire, in a group of freshwater springs. It reaches the Long Island Sound after a journey of 407 miles (655 km).

The first people to inhabit this river valley were Native Americans who hunted caribou, woolly mammoth, and other animals. When the first Europeans came to the valley in the early 1600s, they set up trading posts, then moved farther and farther up the valley into Vermont and New

River: Connecticut

Length: 380 miles (611.5 km)

Distinction: Longest river in New England

Major Tributaries: There are 38 major tributaries

Cities Served by River: Hartford, Springfield, Brattleboro

American Heritage Designated Rivers: Yes

Riverkeeper: No

Watershed: 11,000 square miles (28,490 sq km)

Hampshire, displacing the Native Americans along the way.

Adraien Block was the first European to explore the Connecticut River. Here's what he wrote about the river:

"Next, on the same south coast, succeeds a river named by our countrymen Fresh River, which is shallow at its mouth. . . . In some places it is very shallow, so that at about fifteen leagues [between 30 and 60 miles] up the river there is not much more than five feet of water. There are few inhabitants near the mouth of the river, but at a distance of fifteen leagues above they become more numerous. . . . This river has always a downward current so that no assistance is derived from it in going up, but a favorable wind is necessary." ❧

Captain Block returned to the Netherlands after his voyage and announced that fur trading was possible. Like in New York, the Dutch and Native Americans set up trading in the Connecticut River Valley.

River Rapids

The Connecticut River was rich with populations of shad, Atlantic salmon, and other fish when Captain Block explored the river in the 1600s. A century later, the salmon population was already in question from overfishing. Over the years, the river was dammed and polluted by industry, contributing further to its downfall. In fact, by the mid-1900s it was being called the nation's "best landscaped sewer."

The Federal Clean Water Act of 1972 brought hope to the river. Communities and businesses stopped dumping in the river. The Connecticut River Watershed council was established and worked hard to improve the water quality of the river. Through their efforts and those of other concerned citizens and politicians, the Connecticut River has seen the return of salmon and shad populations.

Fossils and Footprints

In 1800 a student from Williams College found a rock with strange footprints on it in South Hadley, Massachusetts. Other people also began to find strange footprints in Connecticut Valley rocks. Between those footprints, or tracks, and a number of fossils found, scientists have determined what the valley looked like in the Triassic period. Great reptiles, ancestors of the dinosaurs of later periods, walked through a land with giant ferns and evergreens similar to Norfolk pines. Streams meandered through mudflats and became preserved with the footprints. You can see firsthand evidence of this period at Dinosaur State Park in Rocky Hill, Connecticut.

Fossils are fun to look for in the Connecticut Valley. Here are some tips on finding some on your next visit to this area. You can also use these tips when you go fossil hunting in your own backyard.

What You Need
- Paper
- Pencil
- Magnifying glass

What You Do
1. Look at rocky outcroppings (for example, where highways are cut through rock). If you can see the different layers of the rock there might be sandstone or shale. These rocks, known as sedimentary rock, are where most fossils are found. Connecticut was once tropical and evidence of this can be found in fossils of club mosses and horsetails. You might also find fossils of fish. Take a look in old streambeds for dinosaur footprints.

2. A fossil field guide will help you identify what you find. Check out your find with your magnifying glass.

3. When you do find a fossil at a state or national park, look at it, but don't take it with you. Every fossil that is taken out of a park removes important historical and environmental information.

4. Record your find by taking a picture of it or make a rubbing using a pencil and paper.

The Kennebec River

The Kennebec River, originating from Moosehead Lake and the Moose River, flows through the state of Maine. Once a haven for Atlantic salmon, alewives, sturgeon, shad, and striped bass, the river saw these populations destroyed by dams and pollution. Fortunately the Edwards Dam was removed in July 1999. The Kennebec is becoming healthier now that the dam has been removed and there is increased monitoring of the amount of discharge being released into the river.

Check Out Cattails

Have you ever seen the fuzzy brown of a cattail on your river walks? They are tall, narrow-leaved plants that grow in marshes. If you touch the brown fuzz on the top of the plant you'll realize that it is the cattail's seed head. There could be 250,000 seeds in that one seed head, each equipped with a tiny parachute for flying on the wind.

Cattails are perhaps one of the most useful plants to both wildlife and humans. Native Americans and early settlers dried the central part of the root and lower stalk, then ground it up to use for

meal. The actual cattail, or flower, of the plant was roasted and eaten, and the stems were also eaten either raw or boiled. It wasn't uncommon for pioneers and Native Americans to rub the juice from the stems of cattails on their gums to help their

aching teeth. The leaves were used for weaving, for packing material, and for padding seams in boats.

Muskrats build their lodges out of cattails and feed on the young shoots and roots. Beavers and geese also feed on cattails. Many birds, such as bitterns, coots, and red-wing blackbirds, nest among cattails.

Cattails have a unique way of filtering water and help to keep wetlands clean.

Here's a way to take a closer look.

What You Need

- *A grown-up to assist*
- Cattail
- Paper
- Pencil
- Magnifying glass
- Scissors

What You Do

1. Lay the cattail on the table. Take a look at all the parts of the plant. Draw a picture of the cattail plant with your pencil and paper.

2. Gently pull off one of the leaves of the cattail. Look closely at the leaf and where it was attached to the cattail's stalk.

3. Ask a grown-up to cut the leaf in half width-wise. Look at it under your magnifying glass. What shape is the leaf cross section? Draw a picture of what you see.

4. Ask a grown-up to cut the stem in half. What do you see when you look at the cross section under your magnifying glass?

5. Examine the fluff of the cattail. Pull it apart and look at the individual seeds. Take a look under the magnifying glass.

Fighting PCBs

Many rivers in the northeast and other areas are in the midst of raging battles to clean up PCBs. The term PCB has become common in our news and culture, but most people probably don't know what it is. PCB is an abbreviation for *Polychlorinated Biphenyls*, a mixture of dangerous compounds that have been used as coolants and lubricants in transformers, capacitors, and other electrical equipment. They don't burn easily and are good insulators.

River Challenge

Take a closer look at a cross section of a celery stalk and compare it to the cattail leaf. Place the celery in a glass of water with a couple of drops of food coloring. What do you think will happen? Think about how plants like cattails that grow in wetlands can help purify water by absorbing pollution.

PCBs are no longer made in the United States. Their production was stopped in 1977 because there was evidence that because they don't break down in the environment, their buildup can cause health problems. Unfortunately, before production was stopped, PCBs entered the soil, air, and water when they were manufactured, used, and disposed of. Sometimes there were accidental spills and leaks when they were being transported. Sometimes PCBs leak from hazardous waste sites.

When PCBs are in a river they become part of the food chain. Small organisms in the river take them up. Fish and other river creatures eat the smaller organisms, and the PCBs begin to build up in the wildlife of the river. High levels of PCBs in river wildlife are dangerous to the whole ecosystem.

Scientists, corporations, and conservationists have been working for years on the best ways to clean up PCBs from our rivers and communities. They have dredged rivers to scoop them out of the river sediment and experimented with PCB-eating microbes. There is new hope now that an enzyme found in earthworms breaks down PCBs. The riverkeeper of the Housatonic River in Massachusetts is exploring that option for cleaning up the PCBs in that river. More information about this progress can be found at www.housatonic-river.com.

Housatonic Riverkeeper Timothy Gray

Timothy Gray has a degree in Natural Resource Science with a focus on river chemistry and biology. These educational tools have been helpful in Gray's work as the Housatonic riverkeeper. Having lived on the river and heard about the contamination of the river by PCBs, Tim Gray partnered with other University of Massachusetts natural science students, applied for, and received a grant to do the first independent PCB sampling. Their work forced General Electric to undertake one of the largest river cleanups in the world. While Gray wanted to be a musician when he was growing up, he continues to perform professionally and combines this with his love and commitment to this river, which is in his opinion the most gorgeous river in New England.

To find out more about PCBs, kids can go to Health Canada at www.hc-sc.gc.ca/english/iyh/environment/pcb.html. The next activity will show you how you can help with items that are harmful to our environment.

Reduce! Reuse! Recycle!

It pays to reduce, reuse, and recycle. Seventeen trees are saved for every ton of newspaper that is recycled. But not everything is able to be recycled. There are things we throw away all the time that are not biodegradable. This waste will stay in our environment without breaking down. They may not be as dangerous as PCBs, but we can still explore ways to reduce, reuse, and recycle them so that they do not cause any harm to our earth. Here are some ways that you can decrease the amount of trash at your house and help conserve our valuable resources.

What You Need
- *A grown-up to assist*
- Recycle bins
- Marker
- Local community guidelines on recycling

What You Do

1. Contact your town, village, or city government office to find out how to recycle in your area. Most communities have scheduled pick-up times, and all you need to do is sort your recyclables and place them on your curb in bins. Other communities will require you to bring your recyclables to a transfer station. Set up your plastic bins in a basement, garage, or somewhere else that you can store your recyclables and other waste.

2. Label each bin with a marker to indicate what recyclable material you will store in each. For example label one CARDBOARD and PAPER, the next label GLASS, the third PLASTICS, and the last one NON-RECYCLABLES.

3. Ask everyone in your house to put these items in the bins rather than the wastebaskets you might usually use. Ask a grown-up to help you find out how to dispose of each recyclable material when the bins are full.

4. Check into disposal options for non-recyclables, such as printer cartridges, batteries, old eyeglasses, paint, and other items you don't need to throw in the garbage. Many organizations and businesses offer disposal options for these types of waste. The office supply store Staples, for example, offers to collect old printer cartridges for proper disposal. Sometimes you can also find printer cartridge disposal envelopes in post offices and Girl Scout councils.

Recycling Tips and Tricks

1. **You can always recycle newspaper and cardboard.** Tie newspapers with string, or bag them in brown paper bags to dispose of them in your recycle bins. The newspaper that you recycle will be turned back into newspaper. Now that's good news!

2. **Save aluminum soda cans to recycle.** Some of them can be turned right back into cash for you. Check the top or side of the can to see if there is a deposit you can collect in your state. If you can, take the cans to a local supermarket and turn them in for cash. (You can tell if your cans are aluminum if you place a magnet to the side of the can and it doesn't stick to the can.) You can also check with your school principal to discuss starting a school-based recycling program as a fundraising event for school programs.

3. **Glass is completely recyclable.** That means that for every pound of glass you recycle, another pound of glass can be made. All you need to do is rinse out those jars (but be careful to conserve water when doing so) and see if you need to sort the glass by color in your area.

4. **Plastics are a little trickier to recycle.** All of them are recyclable, but they are classified differently. (Note that your local government guidelines will indicate if any plastics are not accepted at this time.) Look at the chart to the right to see how to sort your plastics.

Eyeglasses may be donated to United for Sight or the Lions Club. (See the Resources section for contact information.) Also, check out www.recycleforbreastcancer.org/ and www.recycleforcharity.org/ to find out what other items you can recycle and support a worthy cause.

RECYCLING PLASTICS BY THE NUMBERS

Category	Container Examples
1	Drink bottles and oven-ready meal trays.
2	Bottles for milk and washing-up liquids.
3	Food trays, cling wrap, bottles for mineral water and shampoo.
4	Carrier bags and bin liners.
5	Margarine tubs, microwaveable meal trays.
6	Yogurt containers, Styrofoam meat or fish trays, egg cartons, vending cups, plastic cutlery, protective packaging for electronic goods and toys.
7	Any other plastics that do not fall into any of the above categories. An example is melamine, which is often used in plastic plates and cups.

To the North

It's time to continue our trip north and explore the rivers of Canada—a land of swans, white water, and remote waterways. Are you ready?

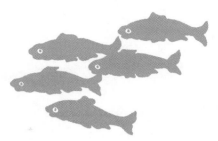

To *the* North

The Greek philosopher Heraclitus may have said those words many centuries ago, but if you listen closely to the song "Just Around the Riverbend" from the movie *Pocahontas* you will hear Pocahontas sing something very similar: "You can't step in the same river twice, the water's always changing, always flowing." What do they mean? If you put your foot into the St. Lawrence River, take it out, and place it back in again, isn't it still the St. Lawrence River? Think about the water that flows over your feet. Where did that water come from, and can you ever touch that water again?

We're going to explore the St. Lawrence River and other rivers of the north in this chapter. We'll find areas that are desolate and wild, areas where swans whistle, and areas that beavers and muskrats call home.

The St. Lawrence River

~~~~~~

Born out of Lake Ontario, the St. Lawrence River flows west to east, connecting the Great Lakes with the Atlantic Ocean. It is called fleuve (FLU-v, meaning "flows to the sea") Saint-Laurent by French Canadians and was known as *Kaniatarowanenneh* (meaning "big waterway") by the native Mohawks.

The first European to explore the river was Jacques Cartier. Roughly a century later in the 17th century, Samuel de Champlain followed Cartier into the St. Lawrence. Champlain took advantage of the abundance of beavers and otters in the area and set up extensive trading between France and Canada. He became known as the father of the fur trade.

River: St. Lawrence

Length: 2,350 miles (3,782 km)

Distinction: Follows fault line

Major Tributaries: Niagara

Cities Served by River: Quebec, Montreal, Rochester, Toronto, Hamilton, Buffalo, Cleveland, Detroit, Chicago, Thunder Bay, Ottawa, Duluth

Watershed: 1,344,000 square miles (3,481,000 sq km)

Zebra Mussels Help Scientists

Could the zebra mussel that is causing havoc in so many North American waterways be useful in any way? Scientists in Canada are making lemonade out of their lemons. In this case their lemons are the zebra mussels in the St. Lawrence River. They have studied zebra mussels in 14 different places in the St. Lawrence River to see if these pests can give them some information on river pollution. They found that the mussels absorb metals and other pollutants from their environment. The populations of mussels in the river contained varying amounts of pollutants, including tin, mercury, and cadmium, depending on their location. This data will help scientists evaluate the St. Lawrence River ecosystem and influence future cleanups.

Turning Lemons into Lemonade

It's time to think like a scientist and see if you can come up with ways that can turn lemons into lemonade, or, in other words, turn problems into solutions for your local river ecosystem.

What You Need
- Paper
- Pencil

What You Do

1. Identify issues affecting your local ecosystems. For example, do you live near wetlands or other habitats threatened by development? Or are there problems with waste disposal in your area? Ask your teacher, scout leader, or parents to help you.

2. Have a brainstorming session with your friends to think of ways to help solve these problems. If there is land threatened by development, can you think of a group that might be interested in purchasing the land and keeping it wild? If there is a waste disposal problem, could you think of ways that recycling could help? A Girl Scout in Chatham, New York, found that there was a problem with the disposal of old mercury thermometers in her area. To complete her requirements for the Gold Award, the highest award in Girl Scouting, she developed a project with a company that would accept the old thermometers and donate new, digital thermometers. See what solutions you can develop.

3. Get help. Find someone to help you make your solutions a reality. You can write a letter to the editor in your local newspaper to offer your suggestions or visit a town meeting with a grown-up. (Also refer to the Resources section in the back of this book for helpful contact information for many river friendly organizations.)

River of Lemonade

Why don't you turn actual lemons into lemonade and set up your own lemonade stand to support your local river? Your contribution might surprise you and your local riverkeeper. Make this simple lemonade and set up a stand. Decide how much to charge for your cups of lemonade. At the end of your sale, bring your money to a local bank and ask for a cashier's check made out to a local environmental action group. If you already know the organization where you'd like to donate your proceeds, you can contact them for brochures or flyers to pass out to your customers.

What You Need

- *A grown-up to assist*
- Saucepan
- 8 cups (1,895 ml) water
- 1¾ cups (350 g) sugar
- Spoon
- Pitcher
- 1½ cups (355 ml) lemon juice
- Paper cups

Yield: 10 8-ounce (236-ml) servings

What You Do

1. Combine the sugar and 1 cup of water in the saucepan.
2. Have a grown-up bring the mixture to a boil and allow the sugar to dissolve. Remove from heat and cool in the refrigerator.

3. Pour the cooled syrup into a pitcher. Add the remaining water and the lemon juice. Make sure your juice is free of pits if you used freshly squeezed juice. Stir and serve.

Beavers

According to many Native American tribes, including the Oneida, Huron, and Iroquois, the beaver dived to the bottom of the sea to fetch mud to build the earth, which shows the animal's importance to the area and its inhabitats. The beaver was once a valuable commodity in North America. Traders like Samuel de Champlain flocked to Canada and other areas in search of pelts for coats, hats, and clothing trim. The furs were shipped to Europe where merchants often paid 10 times the original price. Prior to the demand for beaver pelts, there were an estimated six million beavers in Canada. During the peak of trading, though, 100,000 pelts were being shipped to Europe each year. Thankfully, Europeans took a liking to silk hats and the demand for beaver pelts all but disappeared before the beaver population itself disappeared.

Beavers that live along a river generally build their burrows or holes with an underwater entrance in the riverbank. Those that live in streams, ponds, and lakes usually build a dam that incorporates a lodge. The lodge has a hollow, dry center for raising their young.

The beaver is the national animal of Canada and can be found throughout Canada and the United States, with the exception of most of Florida, most of Nevada, and southern California.

River Challenge

Visit a local nature center or sanctuary. See if you can find evidence of beavers.

Purposeful Pelts

While the thick, glossy coat of the beaver proved to be a valuable commodity to traders, beavers have known all along that their coat was special. Beavers have two layers of fur that contain oil and repel water. The glossy outer coat that we see is made up of guard hairs. Under that coat is another layer of underfur. This layer is so thick that water can't get past it to the beaver's skin. It's like wearing a raincoat over a nice, warm wool coat! Try this experiment to see how this fur works on a beaver's body.

What You Need
- Eyedropper
- Small plate
- Cold water
- Vegetable oil

What You Do

1. Put a few drops of cold water on the plate using the eyedropper.

2. Put a few drops of oil on top of the water. What do you see? The water remains separated from the oil.

3. Shake the plate a little bit and then see what happens to the oil and the water. Does it remain separated?

The oil in the beaver's fur works the same way, keeping the beaver warm and dry.

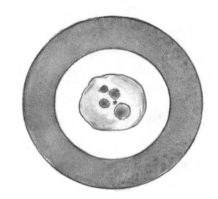

The Mackenzie River

Canada's longest river and perhaps the most remote, the Mackenzie River flows northward into the Arctic Ocean. See if you can find the Mackenzie River on a map of Canada and trace its path with your finger to the cold Arctic Ocean.

The river is named after explorer Alexander Mackenzie, who sailed it in 1789 to find a route to the west coast. Instead, he was disappointed to find the river led north to the Arctic Ocean.

The Mackenzie Muskrats

Muskrats are very flexible animals; they can live just about anywhere from a roadside ditch to an urban swamp. The Mackenzie Delta offers them so much more. The lakes, slow-flowing channels, and willow banks are a virtual five-star habitat for this thick-furred rodent. The muskrat may sometimes share a lodge with a beaver, and they do have thick, waterproof fur similar to beavers, but other than that the two are not closely related. Muskrats are not rats; they are giant field mice that have become adapted to water life. Their tails act like rudders. They can hold their breath for 15 minutes and can chew underwater. They build their lodges from riverbank plants or, if none are available, they burrow into the riverbank.

There are a lot of animals that prey upon muskrats in the delta, including bears, martens, foxes, and mink. Native Americans in this region still trap muskrats for fur and food.

Tundra Swans

You might recognize this swan by the whistle sound it makes with its powerful wings as it flies. In fact, it used to be called the "whistling swan." There are seven species of swan in the world: two of them, the tundra swan and the trumpeter swan, are native to North America. Another swan, the mute swan, is found in North America, but it is not native. It was brought from Europe and Asia years ago.

Trumpeters and tundras look very similar. But if you get close enough, you can see that the tundra swan has a small yellow mark at the base of its bill. They may look alike, but they have very different voices. The trumpeter sounds very much like a trumpet, deep and brassy, while the tundra makes a softer sound.

The tundra swan lives in the tundra of Alaska and Canada during the summer. You might see the

Muskrat

birds wintering on the warmer Atlantic coast, in Chesapeake Bay, or on the coast of California, when the tundra is bitter cold.

Tundra swans have few natural enemies, but they do face problems of pollution, especially in the Chesapeake Bay and lower Great Lakes during migration. The pollution reduces their food supplies. The swans sometimes turn from eating water plants to field grains when they cannot get enough to eat in the water. If crop production is low due to farmland development, for example, the swans will have little to eat. Lower water levels in their migration paths caused by dams and other water diversions also make an impact on their nest building and feeding.

Their breeding grounds are somewhat isolated, which is good, but increased development may have an impact on their short breeding season. Fortunately the swans are rugged birds that have a long lifespan and they are accustomed to some hardships during their life. These magnificent, beloved birds will require careful observation by conservationists.

Tundra Swan

Fascinating Feathers

Swans have different kinds of feathers. Some help them fly and others help them stay warm in the cold tundra weather. Let's see what makes these feathers different.

What You Need
- Assortment of feathers
- Magnifying lens

What You Do
1. Take a look at the different feathers. Do you see one that looks like an old fashioned pen—a quill pen? That is a flight feather.

2. Hold the flight feather in your hand and look at it carefully. You will notice that the flight feather has two *vanes* divided by a shaft. The outer vane is shorter and faces the wind, so it is also very strong. The inner vane is longer and curves up on the end. This vane faces away from the wind and helps keep the bird in the air.

3. Try to pull apart the feather frond. It's tough isn't it? Let's see what is holding it together. Look at the flight feather under your magnifying glass. You will see that there are barbs and barbules, like little hooks, interlocking to form each vane. Looking closely, we can see that there are hooks and catches that lock the feather together.

4. Take a look at a down feather. Those are the fluffy ones that don't have barbules. They are found close to the skin of the bird and keep the bird warm. Do you have down in your pillows, coat, or quilt? They came from geese and provide warmth.

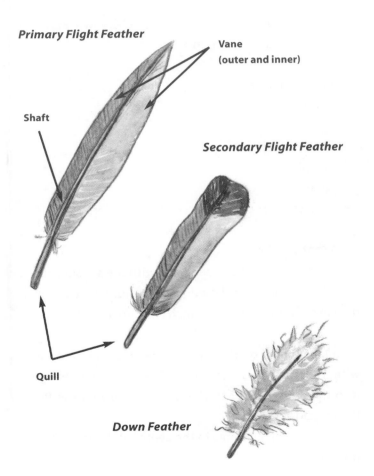

Primary Flight Feather

**Vane
(outer and inner)**

Shaft

Secondary Flight Feather

Quill

Down Feather

White Water 101

Many rivers in North America have what is called *white water*. You probably know what white water is. It's the frothy water that is found in river rapids or waterfalls. Many people love to kayak or raft on white water. If you want to take a tour on your local river, it is important to know the different river classifications. Class I, or easy classification, indicates that the water is flowing smoothly with a few small waves and perhaps some rocks off to the side. This is perfect for a family kayak trip. Class II means that the waves could be about three feet high and you may get a little wet. This is also known as a novice class. Class III means there are small falls, some large rocks, and some big waves. These are for intermediate rafters and not good for a family trip. Kayaking experts enjoy the rough waters of Class IV and V. You'll see turbulent waves, feel a hard current, and face some rocks if you are rafting in Class IV conditions. Steep drops, huge waves, and an even harder current face the expert in Class V conditions. Lastly, Class VI is left only to serious experts. Commercial rafting trips that you might take with your family do not include these areas on their trips.

The Ottawa River

The Ottawa River is one of Canada's major rafting rivers. There are rapids, sandy beaches, and waterfalls. If you are visiting this area be sure to check out the many family rafting tours available.

The Ottawa River was the original trans-Canada highway. First Nations traveled extensively on the river and, when European explorers came to Canada, the Ottawa River served as the "highway" into the interior of Canada. Fur traders traveled from Montreal, up the Ottawa River, and into the Great Lakes and northern rivers. Today the Ottawa River is enjoyed by outdoor enthusiasts for its remaining white water and natural beauty.

River: Ottawa

Length: 789.8 miles (1,271 km)

Major Tributaries: The Gatineau River, the Lievre, the Madawaska (major in terms of size)

Cities Served by River: Ottawa, Gatineau

Riverkeeper: Yes

Watershed: 56,486 square miles (146,300 sq km)

White-Water Riverscape

Here's how to create your own white-water river complete with your own kayak or raft.

What You Need
- Shoebox
- Scissors
- Blue tissue paper
- Pencil
- Glue
- Card stock or oak tag in a variety of colors

What You Do

1. Poke a hole in the shoebox lid with the scissors about ½ inch (1.3 cm) from the edge of the lid. Now cut a window in the lid leaving the ½ inch (1.3 cm) margin from the edge.

2. Place the lid on the tissue paper and trace around it with the pencil. Cut out the completed rectangle and glue it to the underside of the lid to cover the window. Place the lid aside.

3. Cut a small peephole in the center of the small end of the shoebox.

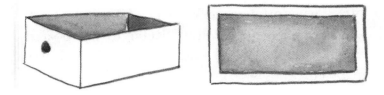

4. Now it is time to create your white-water river. Place the cover gently on the box and take a peek inside through the peephole. The blue tissue paper will let just enough light in to see your river. Start picturing your river inside the box. Glue some blue paper or tissue to the inside of the box to cover the cardboard.

5. Choose the color of your rocks. Think about the class of your river. Is it a Class II with just some rocks on the sides or is it a Class V with many rocks and waterfalls? Rocks come in many different shapes. Cut out at least three rock shapes to fit in your box. Fold down the bottom of the rock shape so that it will be able to stand in your box after it is glued to the bottom.

6. Cut out wave shapes. Glue pieces of white paper to cap them off so that they look like white water. Glue the

first wave toward the front of your box. Continue with more waves until you have filled the box.

7. Look through the peephole while you position them so that you can make sure that you can see them when they are glued.

8. After you have positioned your rocks and waves, cut out your raft or kayak. You can add a person to it by cutting out a small circle face and gluing it inside. Include paddles!

9. Place the lid back on to the box when you have finished. Take a peek. How does your river look?

Ottawa Riverkeeper Meredith Brown

It was in engineering school that Meredith Brown first learned about the impact dams, levees, and other manmade structures have on rivers. She spent five years working for a consulting company in British Columbia to improve fish habitats. She would assess the current conditions of the watershed and the river and make decisions on what natural functions were altered by logging or development. Then a team of engineers, biologists, and ecologists would put together a plan for improving the fish habitat in the river. Sometimes this meant reestablishing native trees along the

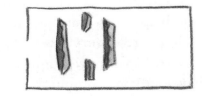

river, removing dams and other obstacles that prevented fish from reaching good spawning habitat, or providing a safe and calm off-channel habitat— a refuge for fish away from the huge flows of the mainstream river. Sometimes it meant reestablishing a series of riffles and pools (slower moving areas of the river where fish can feed and spawn) within the river, repairing eroding banks, or establishing proper meanders and curves in the river.

In this work she learned more about how natural rivers function. She began to realize that protecting rivers was a better course of action than repairing damage caused to a river later. Another riverkeeper was born! Brown has degrees in biology and environmental engineering and a master's degree in resource and environmental management. Brown hates seeing pollution flowing from industries into the river and how poor development practices in the floodplain contribute to a river's problems.

Find out more about how pollution challenges the Ottawa River at the Ottawa Riverkeeper Web site: www.ottawariverkeeper.ca/main.php?op= waterkeeper-proposal.html. Refer to the posted calendar of events to find out how you can get involved.

Bow Riverkeeper Danielle Droitsch

The Bow River is a mountain river formed by the ice-cold water from the Bow Glacier and Rocky Mountain streams, waters from Lake Louise, and white water flowing from a Canadian gorge. Danielle Droitsch knows that her river is very fortunate because it is much cleaner compared to other rivers in North America. But she worries about what will happen to the Bow River in the future. Droitsch points out that the community along the river is growing very, very fast, and scientists are saying that this river is under too much pressure, and now is the time to ensure that this river is clean and protected for the future.

This riverkeeper has a background in law, so she helps make sure people comply with laws to help the river survive.

To learn more about how you help keep the river in your community clean, go to the waterkeeper Web site at: http://waterkeeper.org.

Rock 'n' Roll for Canada's Rivers

The Tragically Hip, a popular Canadian rock band, has teamed up with the Waterkeeper Alliance to help promote water quality protection and Canadians' rights to swim, drink, and fish safely in every community. "I can see communities a hundred years from now—our children's children's children—standing on the banks of their sparkling heritage, beholding the masterpieces waterkeepers helped them win back," says the Tragically Hip's lead singer, Gord Downie.

The band invited Waterkeeper Alliance, which has eight programs in Canada, to introduce its grassroots approach to environmental protection to the band's fans across the country during the Between Evolution tour.

"It excites me to know that people will come to our show, talk to their local waterkeeper, and walk out knowing that the pollution of our national treasures is not only unacceptable, it is reversible," says Downie. The group has a studio located on the shores of Lake Ontario.

Celebrate World Day for Water

In 1992 the United Nations General Assembly declared March 22 of each year to be World Day for Water. It's a day to recognize the importance of water to our well-being, the environmental health and diversity of our planet, energy generation, food production, and industrial development as well as a day to appreciate water's role in the world's cultures and religions. Celebrate the World Day for Water each March 22 in your community by planning a river cleanup with your local riverkeeper organization (see the Resources section for a listing), writing a letter to the editor of your local newspaper about World Day for Water, or visiting the lake, pond, stream, or river near your home to enjoy an afternoon on or beside its waters. Find out more about World Day for Water at www.unesco.org/water/water_celebrations.

Call to Action

This is the end of our river journey. This, however, does not mean it is the end of *your* journey. Your journey will take you to many places. You will see many streams, lakes, and rivers in your lifetime. You will see how fields are irrigated, energy is created, drinkable water is provided, and countless hours of amusement can be enjoyed on waterfronts. Find ways to protect them and preserve their free flowing beauty.

Remember the words of Charles Kuralt at the beginning of this book:

"I started out thinking of America as highways and state lines. As I got to know it better, I began to think of it as rivers." ❦

After reading through these pages, I hope that you, too, think of North America as an area of rivers. I know I do.

Resources

Books, Videos, and Web Sites

CHAPTER 1: THE RIVER HIGHWAY

Books

Boyle, Robert. *The Hudson River: A Natural and Unnatural History.* New York: W. W. Norton & Company, 1979.

Wick, Walter. *A Drop of Water: A Book of Science and Wonder.* New York: Scholastic, 1997.

Web Sites

Visit the Hudson River Fishermen's Association at www.hrfanj.org.

CHAPTER 2:
RIDE THE RAPIDS OF THE WESTERN RIVERS

Books

Copeland, Peter. *Powell's Colorado River Expedition Coloring Book.* New York: Dover Publications, 1993.

Weisheit, John. *Cataract Canyon: A Human and Environmental History of the River and Canyon Lands.* Salt Lake City: University of Utah Press, 2004.

Web Sites

Learn about the Sacramento River Watershed Program at www.sacriver.org.

Visit the Colorado Riverkeeper at www.livingrivers.org.

Learn more about the Atlas Corporation cleanup at www.grandcanyontrust.org/arches/atlas/science.html.

See what Waterkeeper Alliance is doing about mercury levels in our rivers at http://waterkeeper.org/mainarticle details.aspx?articleid=84.

Read more about the Rivers Unplugged Campaign of American Rivers at www.amrivers.org/index.php?module =HyperContent&func=displayview&shortname=riversun plugged.

Order a gold panning kit from the Mineral Information Institute (www.mii.org/panforgold.html) and find places to pan at www.goldmaps.com.

Learn more about the colors and karats of gold at the World Gold Council site, www.gold.org/jewellery/technol ogy/colours/index.html.

Find out more about the American Land Conservancy at www.alcnet.org/alc-home.php.

CHAPTER 3:
THE GREAT RIVERS OF THE NORTHWEST

Books

Cole, Joanna. *Magic School Bus Goes Upstream: A Book About Salmon on Migration.* New York: Scholastic, 1997.

Cone, Molly. *Come Back, Salmon: How a Group of Dedicated Kids Adopted Pigeon Creek and Brought It Back to Life.* San Francisco: Sierra Club Books for Children, 1994.

Web Sites

Look at the Columbia River at the National Geographic site at www.nationalgeographic.com/earthpulse/columbia/index_flash.html.

Take the Salmon Challenge at the American Rivers site at http://dnr.metrokc.gov/wlr/waterres/salmonch.htm.

Print out the U.S. Fish and Wildlife's salmon coloring book at http://pacific.fws.gov/publications/salmnbk.pdf.

Video/DVD

A River Runs Through It. DVD. Directed by Robert Redford. 1992; Columbia/Tristar Home Video, 2002.

CHAPTER 4:
RIVERS OF THE SOUTHWEST

Web Sites

Learn more Spanish at the Enchanted Learning Spanish pages at www.enchantedlearning.com/themes/Spanish.shtml.

Look up your state seal at www.netstate.com/states/index.html.

Show your support for the Gila River by contacting

Governor Bill Richardson
State Capitol, Room 240
Santa Fe, NM 87501
(505) 476-2200
Fax: (505) 476-2226
E-mail form available on www.governor.state.nm.us.

Senator Jeff Bingaman
(202) 224-5521
Fax: (202) 224-2852
senator_bingaman@bingaman.senate.gov

Senator John McCain
(202) 224-2235
Fax: (202) 228-2862
http://mccain.senate.gov/

CHAPTER 5: LIFE ON THE MISSISSIPPI, MISSOURI, AND OTHER MIDWEST RIVERS

Books

Eubank, Patricia Reeder. *Seaman's Journal: On the Trail with Lewis and Clark.* Nashville, TN: Ideals Children's Books, 2002.

Herbert, Janis. *Lewis and Clark for Kids.* Chicago: Chicago Review Press, 2000.

Video/DVD

The Adventures of Huck Finn. DVD. Directed by Stephen Sommers. 1993; Buena Vista Home Video, 2003.

Web Sites

If you live near the Mississippi River, check out the Mississippi Passport program to find great family activities for exploring the river at www.mississippipassport.org.

Check out a map that shows the distribution of zebra mussels in the United States at http://nationalatlas.gov/zmussels1.html.

CHAPTER 6: "SHOOT THE HOOCH" AND OTHER FUN ON SOUTHEASTERN RIVERS

Books

Grahame, Kenneth. *The Wind in the Willows.* New York: Harcourt, 2002.

Multimedia

Waters to the Sea. CD-ROM, http://cgee.hemline.edu/waters2thesea/Chattahoochee.

Video/DVD

Ring of Bright Water. DVD. Directed by Jack Couffer. 1969; Culver City, CA: Columbia/Tristar Home Video, 2004.

Web Sites

Play the otter games at the American Rivers site, found at www.twingroves.district96.k12.il.us/Wetlands/Wetland Games/Ottergy/Ottergy.html and www.twingroves.district96.k12.il.us/Wetlands/WetlandGames/RiverOtter Game/RiverOtterGame.html.

See steamboats of the 50 states at www.steamboats.com/research/50states.html.

CHAPTER 7: RIVERS OF THE NORTHEAST

Books

Baron, Robert, and Thomas Locker. *Hudson: The Story of a River*. Golden, CO: Fulcrum Publishing, 2004.

Cherry, Lynne. *A River Ran Wild: An Environmental History*. New York: Harcourt Brace / Gulliver Green, 1992.

Hanrahan, Brendan. *Great Day Trips in the Connecticut Valley of the Dinosaurs*. Wilton, CT: Perry Heights Press, 2004.

Thompson, Ida. *National Audubon Society Field Guide to North American Fossils*. New York: Alfred A. Knopf, 1982.

Web Sites

Share your observations with other Hudson River lovers by e-mailing them to the Hudson River E-Almanac at trlake7@aol.com by 9:00 P.M. on the Monday previous to publication. The Hudson River E-Almanac is compiled and edited by Tom Lake and e-mailed weekly by DEC's Hudson River Estuary Program. To sign up to receive the E-Almanac, send an e-mail message to hrep@gw.dec.state.ny.us and write "E-Almanac" in the subject line.

Take a look at Bannerman Castle photos and history at www.bannermancastle.org.

Visit the Connecticut River Watershed Council's Web site at www.ctriver.org.

Eyeglass donations can be made to United for Sight at www.uniteforsight.org or to Lions Clubs International at www.lionsclubs.org/EN/content/vision_eyeglass_sight.shtml. Also check with your local Goodwill Industries location to see if they have an eyeglass donation receptacle.

CHAPTER 8: TO THE NORTH

Web Sites

Beaver Coloring pages
Print out blackline drawings of beavers to color in at www.first-school.ws/theme/animals/cp_wild/cp_beaver.htm.

Girl Scouts of the USA and Girl Guides of Canada
www.girlscouts.org
www.girlguides.ca.

The Tragically Hip
www.thehip.com
You'll find information on their Web site for the Waterkeeper Alliance, a grassroots organization with 132 local waterkeeper programs. Look up your local riverkeeper or waterkeepers on their site. More details: http://waterkeeper.org.

Riverkeepers and Other Waterkeepers

⊚ denotes a riverkeeper included in this book

CANADA

⊚ **Bow Riverkeeper, Danielle Droitsch, Esq.**
P.O. Box 3120
Banff , Alberta T1L 1C7
(403) 762-0591
www.bowriverkeeper.org

Canadian Detroit Riverkeeper
2710 Robert Road
Windsor, Ontario N9A 2L9
(519) 257-2413

Fraser Riverkeeper
1204-1251 Cardero Street
Vancouver, British Columbia V6G 2H9
(604) 838-1584
www.fraserriverkeeper.ca

Fundy Baykeeper
Conservation Council of New Brunswick
45 Libby Lane
Waweig, New Brunswick E3L521
(506) 466-4033
www.web.net/~ccnb

Georgian Baykeeper
Georgian Bay Area Foundation
19 Edgecombe Ave.
Toronto, Ontario M5N 2X1
(416) 489-8101
www.georgianbay.ca

Lake Ontario Waterkeeper
245 Queen's Quay West
Toronto, Ontario M5J 2K9
(416) 861-1237
www.waterkeeper.ca

⊚ **Ottawa Riverkeeper, Meredith Brown**
P.O. Box 67008
421 Richmond Rd.
Ottawa, Ontario K2A 4E4
(613) 864-7442, 1-888-9KEEPER
www.ottawariverkeeper.ca

Petitcodiac Riverkeeper, Inc./ Sentinelles de la Rivière Petitcodiac, Inc.
P.O. Box 300
Moncton, New Brunswick E1C 8K9
(506) 388-5337
www.petitcodiac.org

MEXICO AND SOUTH AMERICA

Colombian Amazonia Waterkeeper
Carrera 97 #62-97
Bogota, DC
Colombia
(571) 491-5071

Choqueyapu Riverkeeper
Av. Arce, 2300 Edificio Amazonas
Piso 9, Dpto. 901 Cx. P.-1182
Bairro Sopocachi
La Paz
Bolivia
(591) 719-69858

Magdalena Baykeeper
Center for Coastal Studies, AP. 15
Pto. San Carlos, BCS, 23740
Mexico
(52) 613-1360548

Punta Abreojos Coastkeeper
Domocilio Conocido
Punta Abreojos, BCS,
Mexico
(52) 615-15-620-53

Rio Hondo Riverkeeper
Av. Juan Jose Siordia 297
Esquina Emiliano Zapata. Col.
  Leona Vicario
Chetumal, Quintana Roo,
Mexico
(52) 983-83-25543

UNITED STATES

Alabama

Black Warrior Riverkeeper
P.O. Box 59684
Birmingham, AL 35259
(205) 458-0095
www.blackwarriorriver.org

Choctawhatchee Riverkeeper
207 Gail Street
Troy, AL 36079
(334) 670-3624

Hurricane Creekkeeper
Friends of Hurricane Creek
5600 Holt-Peterson Road
Tuscaloosa, AL 35404
(205) 507-0867
www.hurricanecreek.org

Mobile Baykeeper
Mobile Bay Watch, Inc.
5 North Jackson Street
Mobile, AL 36602
(251) 433-4229
www.mobilebaywatch.org

Village Creekkeeper
Village Creek Human &
Environmental Justice Society
P.O. Box 310715
Birmingham, AL 35231
(205) 798-0087

Alaska

Prince William Soundkeeper
P.O. Box 2832
Valdez, AK 99686
(907) 272-0502

Arizona

Black Mesa Waterkeeper
Black Mesa Trust
P.O. Box 30456
Flagstaff, AZ 86003-0456
(928) 734-9255
www.blackmesatrust.org

California

Baja California Coastkeeper
Wildcoast
925 Seacoast Drive
Imperial Beach, CA 91932
(619) 423-8665 ext. 202
www.wildcoast.net

Baykeeper
55 Hawthorne Street,
  Suite 550
San Francisco, CA 94105-3924
(415) 856-0444
www.baykeeper.org

California Coastkeeper Alliance
P.O. Box 3156
Fremont, CA 92106
(510) 770-9764
www.cacoastkeeper.org

Humboldt Baykeeper
424 First Street
Eureka, CA 95501
(707) 268-0664
www.humboldtbaykeeper.org

Orange County Coastkeeper
441 Newport Blvd., Suite 103
Newport Beach, CA 92663
(949) 723-5424
www.coastkeeper.org

Petaluma Riverkeeper
Waterkeepers Northern California
521 Walnut Street
Petaluma, CA 94952
(707) 763-7756
www.baykeeper.org

Russian Riverkeeper
Friends of the Russian River
P.O. Box 1335
Healdsburg, CA 95448
(707) 433-1958
www.russianriverkeeper.org

**Sacramento-San Joaquin
Deltakeeper**
Waterkeepers Northern California
3536 Rainer Ave.

Stockton, CA 95204
(209) 464-5090
www.baykeeper.org

San Diego Coastkeeper
2924 Emerson Street, Suite 220
San Diego, CA 92106
(619) 758-7743
www.sdbaykeeper.org

San Francisco Baykeeper
Waterkeepers Northern California
55 Hawthorne St., Suite 550
San Francisco, CA 94015
(415) 856-0444
www.baykeeper.org

San Luis Obispo (SLO) Coastkeeper
Environment in the Public Interest
  EPI-Center
1013 Monterey St., Suite 207
San Luis Obispo, CA 93401
(805) 781-9932
www.epicenteronline.org

Santa Barbara Channelkeeper
714 Bond Street
Santa Barbara, CA 93103
(805) 563-3377
www.sbck.org

Santa Monica Baykeeper
P.O. Box 10096
Marina del Rey, CA 90295
(310) 305-9645
www.smbaykeeper.org

Ventura Coastkeeper
Wishtoyo Foundation
3600 South Harbor Blvd, Suite 222
Oxnard, CA 93035
(805) 382-4540
www.wishtoyo.org

Colorado

Alamosa Riverkeeper
Valle de Sol Community Center
P.O. Box 223
Capulin, CO 81124
(719) 274-4298

Connecticut

Long Island Soundkeeper
Soundkeeper, Inc.
P.O. Box 4058
East Norwalk, CT 06855
(203) 854-5330
www.soundkeeper.org

District of Columbia

Anacostia Riverkeeper
Earth Conservation Corps
First St. & Potomac Ave., SE
Washington, DC 20003
(202) 554-1960 ext. 215
www.anacostiariverkeeper.org

Florida

Apalachicola Bay and Riverkeeper
P.O. Box 484
Eastpoint, FL 32328
(850) 670-5470
www.abark.org

Indian Riverkeeper
Treasure Coast Environmental
    Defense Fund
10303 S. Indian River Drive
Ft. Pierce, FL 34982
(772) 336-7284
www.geocities.com/RainForest/
    jungle/9343/

Pensacola Gulf Coastkeeper
P.O. Box 13283
Pensacola, FL 32591
(850) 429-8422
www.coastkeepers.org

St. John's Riverkeeper
Jacksonville University
2800 University Blvd. N
Jacksonville, FL 32211
(904) 256-7591
www.stjohnsriverkeeper.org

Wakulla/Aucilla Waterkeeper
Florida Wildlife Federation
56 Red Bud Lane
Crawfordville, FL 32327
 (850) 942-0990

Georgia

**Altamaha Riverkeeper and
Coastkeeper**
P.O. Box 2642
Darien, GA 31305
(912) 437-8164
www.altamahariverkeeper.org

Canoochee Riverkeeper
P.O. Box 263
Swainsboro, GA 30401
(478) 289-6523
www.canoocheeriverkeeper.org

⊛ **Chattahoochee Riverkeeper,
Jim Phillips**
P.O. Box 1492
Columbus, GA 31902
(706) 317-4837
www.theriverwatch.org

Ocmulgee Riverkeeper
817 Mulberry St.
Macon, GA 31201
(912) 437-8164
www.ocumulgee.org

Satilla Riverkeeper
P.O. Box 177
Waynesville, GA 31566
(912) 223-6761
grogers1@btconline.net.

Savannah Riverkeeper
1226 River Ridge Road
Augusta, GA 30909
(706) 364-5253
www.savannahriverkeeper.org

⊛ **Upper Chattahoochee
Riverkeeper, Sally Bethea**
3 Puritan Mill, 916 Joseph
    Lowery Blvd.
Atlanta, GA 30318

(404) 352-9828

www.chattahoochee.org

Upper Coosa Riverkeeper

Coosa River Basin Initiative

408 Broad Street

Rome, GA 30161

(706) 232-2724

www.coosa.org

Indiana

Wabash Riverkeeper

1915 West 18th Street

Indianapolis, IN 46202

(317) 685-8800

http://www.hecweb.org/Wabash%2
  0Riverkeeper/wabash_riverkeeper
  _index.htm

Kansas

**Kansas Riverkeeper/Friends of
the Kaw**

Kansas Riverkeeper, Inc.

P.O. Box 1612

Lawerence, KS 66044

(785) 312-7200

www.kansasriver.com

Kentucky

Kentucky Riverkeeper

300 Summit Street

Richmond, KY 40475

(859) 622-1622

www.kentuckyriverkeeper.org

Louisiana

Atchafalaya Basinkeeper

32675 Gracie Ln. Unit D

Plaquemine, LA 70764

(225) 659-2499

Louisiana Bayoukeeper

4927 Deborah Ann Drive

Barataria, LA 70036

(504) 689-7880

◉ **Lower Mississippi Riverkeeper,
Mary Lee Orr**

Louisiana Environmental Action
  Network

P.O. Box 66323

Baton Rouge, LA 70896

(225) 928-1315

www.leanweb.org

Maine

Casco Baykeeper

Friends of Casco Bay

2 Fort Road

South Portland, MN 04106

(207) 799-8574

www.cascobay.org

Maryland

Assateague Coastkeeper

Assateague Coastal Trust

P.O. Box 731

Berlin, MD 21811

(410) 629-7538

www.actforbays.org

Chester Riverkeeper

Chester River Association

100 N. Cross St., Suite 1

Chestertown, MD 21620

(410) 810-7556

www.chesterriverassociation.org

Patapsco Riverkeeper

4798 Roundhill Road

Ellicott City, MD 21043

(410) 313-8826

www.patapscoriverkeeper.org

Patuxent Riverkeeper
18600 Queen Anne Road, Rear Barn
Upper Marlboro, MD 20774
(301) 249-8200
www.paxriverkeeper.org

Potomac Riverkeeper, Inc.
P.O. Box 1164
Rockville, MD 20849
(202) 222-0777
www.potomacriverkeeper.org

Severn Riverkeeper
Chesapeake Rivers Association
329 Riverview Trail
Annapolis, MD 21401
(410) 849-8540

South Riverkeeper
South River Federation
6 Herndon Dr.
Annapolis, MD 21403
(443) 482-2154
www.southriverfederation.net

West/Rhode Riverkeeper, Inc.
1456 East West Shady Side Rd.
Shady Side, MD 20764
(301) 261-5021

Massachusetts

Buzzards Baykeeper
Coalition for Buzzards Bay
620 Belleville Ave.
New Bedford, MA 02745
(508) 999-6363
www.savebuzzardsbay.org

⊙ **Housatonic Riverkeeper,
Timothy Gray**
Housatonic River Initiative
P.O. Box 321
Lenoxdale, MA 01242
(413) 243-3353
www.housatonic-river.com

Nantucket Soundkeeper
396 Main St., Suite #2
Hyannis, MS 02601
(508) 775-9767
www.saveoursound.org

Michigan

Detroit Riverkeeper
Friends of the Detroit River
3020 Oakwood Street
Melvindale, MI 48122
(734) 676-4626
www.detroitriver.org

Grand Traverse Baykeeper
The Watershed Center Grand
    Traverse Bay
232 E. Front Street
Traverse City, MI 49684
(231) 935-1514
www.gtbay.org

Muskegon Riverkeeper
6112 E. 86th Street
Newyago, MI 49337
(231) 652-6594

St. Clair Channelkeeper
38217 Cherry Lane
Harrison TWP, MI 48045
(586) 764-2443

Tip of the Mitt Waterkeeper
Tip of the Mitt Watershed Council
Petoskey, MI 49770
(231) 347-1181 ext.114
www.watershedcouncil.org

New Jersey

Hackensack Riverkeeper
231 Main Street
Hackensack, NJ 07601
(201) 968-0808
www.hackensackriverkeeper.org

New York/New Jersey Baykeeper
52 West Front Street
Keyport, NJ 07735
(732) 888-9870
www.nynjbaykeeper.org

Raritan Riverkeeper
P.O. Box 244
Keasbey, NJ 08832
(732) 442-6313
www.nynjbaykeeper.org

New York

Buffalo Niagara Riverkeeper
616 Potomac Avenue
Buffalo, NY 14222
(716) 881-1217
www.fbnr.org

Erie Canalkeeper
73 Valleyview Drive
Brockport, NY 14420
(585) 576-8092
www.eriecanalkeeper.org

◉ **Hudson Riverkeeper,**
Alex Matthiessen
P.O. Box 130
Garrison, NY 10524

(845) 424-4149
www.riverkeeper.org

Lake George Waterkeeper
Fund for Lake George
P.O. Box 1231
Bolton Landing, NY 12814
(518) 644-5337
www.lakegeorgewaterkeeper.org

Peconic Baykeeper
P.O. Box 1308
Riverhead, NY 11901
(631) 727-7346
www.peconicbaykeeper.org

Upper St. Lawrence Riverkeeper
Save the River!
409 Riverside Drive
Clayton, NY 13624
(315) 686-2010

North Carolina

Cape Fear Coastkeeper
North Carolina Coastal Federation-
   Field Office
3806-B Park Avenue
Wilmington, NC 28403
(910) 790-3275
www.nccoast.org

Cape Fear Riverkeeper
Cape Fear Riverwatch
617 Surry Street
Wilmington, NC 28401
(910) 762-5606
http://cfrw.us

Cape Hatteras Coastkeeper
P.O. Box 475
Manteo, NC 27954
(252) 473-1607

Cape Lookout Coastkeeper
North Carolina Coastal Federation
3609 Highway 24
Newport, NC 28570
(252) 393-8185
www.nccoast.org

Catawba Riverkeeper
Catawba River Foundation, Inc.
The Great Aunt Stella Center,
   Suite 301
926 Elizabeth Ave.
Charlotte, NC 28204
(704) 679-9494
www.catawbariverkeeper.org

French Broad Riverkeeper
170 Lyman Street
Asheville, NC 28801

(828) 252-8474

www.riverlink.org

Lower Neuse Riverkeeper
Neuse River Foundation
P.O. Box 15451
New Bern, NC 28561
(252) 637-1970
www.neuseriver.org/RiverKeeper.
 html

New Riverkeeper
New River Foundation, Inc.
P.O. Box 241
Jacksonville, NC 28541-0241
(910) 389-6765
www.newriverfoundation.org

Pamlico-Tar Riverkeeper
Pamlico-Tar River Foundation
P.O. Box 1854
Washington, NC 27889
(252) 946-7211
www.ptrf.org

Upper Neuse Riverkeeper
Neuse River Foundation
112 South Blount Street
Raleigh, NC 27601
(919) 856-1180
www.neuseriver.org

Ohio

Clinton Streamkeeper
885 Spencer Road
Sabina, OH 45169
(937) 584-2843

Lake Erie Waterkeeper, Western Basin
6565 Bayshore Rd.
Oregon, OH 43618
(419) 691-3788
www.westernlakeerie.org

Oklahoma

Grand Riverkeeper, Oklahoma
LEAD Agency, Inc.
19257 S. 4403 Dr
Vinita, OK 74301
(918) 256-5269
www.leadagency.org

Oregon

Tualatin Riverkeepers
16507 SW Roy Rogers Rd.
Sherwood, OR 97140
(503) 590-5813
www.tualatinriverkeepers.org

Willamette Riverkeeper
380 SE Spokane Street, Suite 305
Portland, OR 97202
(503) 223-6418
www.willamette-riverkeeper.org

Pennsylvania

Allegheny Riverkeeper
American Littoral Society
48 Center Avenue
West View, PA 15229

Delaware Riverkeeper
Delaware Riverkeeper Network
P.O. Box 326
Washington Crossing, PA 18977
(215) 369-1188
www.delawareriverkeeper.org

Monongahela Riverkeeper
Monongahela River Society
28 Church Street
Waynesburg, PA 15370
(724) 627-6166
www.monriverkeeper.org

Upper Susquehanna Riverkeeper
Tioga Watershed Reclamation
 Project, Inc.

763 S. Main St.
Mansfield, PA 16933
(570) 662-3624

Yough Riverkeeper
Mountain Watershed Association
P.O. Box 408
Melcroft, PA 15462
(724) 455-4200
www.mtwatershed.com

Rhode Island

Narragansett Baykeeper
Save the Bay
434 Smith Street
Providence, RI 02906
(401) 272-3540
www.savebay.org

South Carolina

Waccamaw Riverkeeper
Coastal Carolina University Center
   for Marine and Wetland Studies
1270 Atlantic Ave.
Conway, SC 29526
(843) 349-4007
www.winyahrivers.org

Tennessee

Tennessee Riverkeeper
Broadened Horizons Riverkeeper
   Project
P.O. Box 90
Sale Creek, TN 37373
(423) 332-0748

Texas

Galveston Baykeeper
Galveston Bay Conservation and
   Preservation Association
P.O. Box 323
Seabrook, TX 77586
(281) 326-3343
www.gbcpa.net

Utah

◉ **Colorado Riverkeeper, John Weisheit**
Living Rivers
P.O. Box 466
Moab, UT 84532
(435) 259-1063
www.coloradoriverkeeper.org

Great Salt Lakekeeper
P.O. Box 522220
Salt Lake City, UT 84152
(801) 485-2550
www.greatsaltlakekeeper.org

Vermont

Lake Champlain Lakekeeper
Conservation Law Foundation
15 East State Street, Suite 4
Montpelier, VT 05602
(802) 223-5992
www.clf.org/lakekeeper/press.htm

Virginia

Blackwater/Nottoway Riverkeeper
P.O. Box 44
Sedley, VA 23878
(757) 562-5173
www.blackwaternottoway.com

◉ **James Riverkeeper, Charles Frederickson**
James River Association
P.O. Box 909
Mechanicsville, VA 23110
(804) 733-6820
www.jamesriverassociation.org

Virginia Eastern Shorekeeper

P.O. Box 961

Eastville, VA 23347

(757) 678-6182

Washington

◉ **Columbia Riverkeeper,
Greg deBruler**

P.O. Box 912

Bingen, WA 98605

(509) 493-2808

www.columbiariverkeeper.org

Commencement Baykeeper

Citizens for a Healthy Bay

917 Pacific Avenue #100

Tacoma, WA 98402

(253) 383-2429

www.healthybay.org

North Sound Baykeeper

1155 N. State Street, Suite 623

Bellingham, WA 98225

(360) 733-8307

www.re-sources.org

Puget Soundkeeper

Puget Soundkeeper Alliance

5309 Shilshole Ave. NW, Suite 215

Seattle, WA 98107

(206) 297-7002

www.pugetsoundkeeper.org

West Virginia

**West Virginia Headwaters
Waterkeeper**

HC 78

Box 227

Rock Cave, WV 26234

(304) 924-5802

Wisconsin

Lake Superior Waterkeeper

P.O. Box 33

Ashland, WI 54806

(866) 296-5253

www.superioralliance.org

Milwaukee Riverkeeper

Friends of Milwaukee's Rivers

1845 N. Farwell Ave., Suite 100

Milwaukee, WI 53202

(414) 287-0207 ext. 29

www.mkeriverkeeper.org

Places to Visit

~~~~~~~~~~~~~~~~~

Arizona

Casa Grande Ruins National Monument
1100 Ruins Drive
Coolidge, AZ 85228
(520) 723-3172
www.nps.gov/cagr/pphtml/
   planyourvisit.html
Gila River Heritage Theme Park features self-guided tours of traditional Indian homes of the Pima, Maricopa, Tohono O'odham, and Apache tribes.

California

Columbia State Historic Park
Highway 49
Columbia, CA 95310
(209) 532-4301
Sign up for tours and gold panning lessons.

Marshall Gold Discovery State Historic Park
Highway 49
Coloma, CA 95613
(916) 622-3470
Gold pans are sold at the visitors center.

South Yuba River State Park Project
Bridgeport Covered Bridge
Pleasant Valley Road
Penn Valley, CA 95946
(916) 432-2546
Gold pans are available for loan here; ask about the demonstrations, too.

Sutter Gold Mine
13660 Highway 49,
Sutter Creek, CA 95685
www.caverntours.com/
   sgmt.html
This is the site of the original gold rush. Try your hand at panning for gold or gemstone mining.

The Spirit of Sacramento Riverboat Cruises
110 L Street
Old Sacramento, CA 95814
(800) 433-0263

Colusa-Sacramento River State Recreation Area
Sacramento River
   Discovery Center
Red Bluff, CA 96080
(530) 527-1196
North of Sacramento, take Hwy 20 east for nine miles to Colusa. The park is located near downtown Colusa.

Salmon Viewing Area
Sale Lane
Red Bluff, CA 96080
(530) 527-3043

Sacramento River National Wildlife Refuge
http://refuges.fws.gov/pro
   files/
   index.cfm?id=11627
(530) 934-2801

Connecticut

Connecticut River
Participate in a river clean-up along the Connecticut River and local tributaries. Call the Connecticut River Watershed Council for information at (413) 772-2020.

Delaware

Upper Delaware National Park
274 River Road
Beach Lake, PA 18405
(570) 685-4871
www.nps.gov/upde/
   index.htm

Georgia

Chattahoochee Nature Center
9135 Willeo Road
Roswell, GA 30075
(770) 992-2055
www.chattnature
   center.com

Illinois

The Notebaert Nature Center
2430 N. Cannon Drive
Chicago, IL 60614
(773) 755-5100
www.naturemuseum.org
They have a permanent exhibit on rivers.

Iowa

National Mississippi River Museum and Aquarium
Dubuque, IA
(800) 226-3369
www.rivermuseum.com

Minnesota

Mississippi National River and Recreation Area
Mississippi River
   Visitor Center
120 Kellogg Boulevard West
St. Paul, MN 55102
(651) 293-0200

New Mexico

The Rio Grande Nature Center
2901 Candelaria Road NW
Albuquerque, NM 87107
www.emnrd.state.nm.us/
   nmparks/PAGES/PARKS/
   RGNC/RGNC.HTM

New York

Bannerman Castle
Tour the island by boat on the Pride of the Hudson. Reservations are recommended.
Call Lynne Kirschhoffer at (845) 220-2120 or www.bannermancastle.org/
   news.html for schedule.

Hudson River Islands State Park
1 Hailes Cave Road
Voorheesville, NY 12186
(518) 872-1237

Corning Preserve
West side of Hudson River
Albany, NY 12207

North Carolina

Reed Gold Mine
9621 Reed Mine Road
Midland, NC 28107
(704) 721-GOLD

Oregon

Lewis & Clark State Recreation Site
Off Interstate 84, 16 miles east of Portland, OR
(800) 551-6949

South Dakota

Missouri National Recreational River
P.O. Box 666
Yankton, SD 57078
Visitor Information:
   (402) 667-2550

Texas

Brazos Bend State Park
21901 FM 762
Needville, TX 77461
(979) 553-5101

www.llbean.com/
   parksearch/parks/html/
   837lls.htm

Wyoming

Snake River Kayak & Canoe
P.O. Box 4311
365 N. Cache Street
Jackson Hole, WY 83001
(307) 733-9999 or (800)
   KAYAK-01
(800) 529-2501
www.snakeriverkayak.com

CANADA

Montreal

Biosphère
160, chemin Tour-de-l'Isle
Île Sainte-Hélène
Montreal (Quebec)
H3C 4G8
Canada
(514) 283-5000
www.biosphere.ec.gc.ca

Organizations

~~~~~~

American Rivers

1025 Vermont Ave NW, Suite 720

Washington, DC 20005

(202) 347-7550

Fax: (202) 347-9240

amrivers@amrivers.org

American Rivers is a national non-profit conservation organization dedicated to protecting and restoring healthy natural rivers and the variety of life they sustain for people, fish, and wildlife.

The Hudson River Estuary Program

NYS Department of Environmental Conservation, Region 3

21 South Putt Corners Road

New Paltz, NY 12561

(845) 256-3016

Fax: (845) 255-3649

hrep@gw.dec.state.ny.us

The Hudson River Estuary Program is a unique regional partnership managed by the New York State Department of Environmental Conservation designed to protect, conserve, restore, and enhance the estuary of the Hudson River. The NYS DEC works with local governments and many different organizations, including New York State's Office of Parks, Recreation and Historic Preservation, Department of State, Office of General Services, and Department of Transportation, the Metro-North Railroad, the Hudson River Greenway, the Hudson River Foundation, and Cornell University.

The National Organization for Rivers (NORS)

Membership Offices: 212 W. Cheyenne Mountain Boulevard

Colorado Springs, CO 80906

(719) 579-8759

Fax: (719) 576-6238

nationalrivers@email.msn.com

The National Organization for Rivers (NORS) focuses on canoeing, kayaking, rafting, fly-fishing, river conservation, river access, and river navigability law.

Waterkeeper Alliance

828 South Broadway, Suite 100

Tarrytown, NY 10591

(914) 674-0622

info@waterkeeper.org

A grassroots organization with 132 local waterkeeper programs. Look up your local riverkeeper or waterkeepers on their site. Details at http://waterkeeper.org.

Calendar of Events

April

Beginning in April Family Canoe Trips

Explore the ecology of wetlands typically found around the Chesapeake Bay. Find out how wetlands help fish and crabs living in the bay and how scientists study this type of ecosystem. Sponsored by the Smithsonian Environmental Research Center. For information www.serc.si.edu/education/canoeing/index.htm or call (443) 482-2218.

End of April Mississippi Flyway Birding Festival

Join birders in Wisconsin for a celebration of the spring bird migration. There are seminars and activities to welcome the birds back to the region. For more information go to http://couleeaudubon.org/festival04.html.

May

Holyoke Gas & Electric's Annual Shad Derby

Fish for shad at one of the world's premier fishin' spots. Win prizes for your catch. Registration required. See www.hged.com or call Cal Chunglo (413) 536-9461.

Run with the Alewives

This is an annual favorite for all ages. Learn all about this famous alewife run and its distinguished history. If the alewife cooperate, and they most always do, you will witness one of New England's most spectacular fish runs. Join trip leader Pete Noyes at the fish ladder off the Mills Road in Damariscotta Mills at 10:00 A.M. For additional info check the Damariscotta River Association's Web site calendar at www.draclt.org.

Memorial Day Weekend Annual Sail the Hudson River Highlands

Clearwater and the schooner *Mystic Whaler* host six-hour sails on Saturday and Sunday of the holiday weekend. Sail the Hudson River Highlands, one America's most dramatic landscapes. Call (800) 697-8420.

Memorial Day through Labor Day

Sail on the Tennessee River aboard the Southern Belle Riverboat. It sails from Chattanooga, Tennessee. Check it out at www.chattanoogariverboat.com.

June

Connecticut RiverFest, in Wilder, Vermont

This festival features exhibits, paddling, food, dance, music, and fun for the whole family. Go to www.ctriverfest.org or call (802) 333-3549 for more details.

Clearwater Festival, New York

Annual festival with music www.clearwater.org and www.clearwaterfestival.org.

July

Weekends, Tuber's Cruise on the James River

Float down the James River in an inner tube and enjoy the river up close and personal! Contact Ralph White at James River Park at (804) 646-8911 for more information.

Annual Hudson River Paddle in New York State

Celebrate the Hudson River by paddling south from Albany or visit one of the festivals along the shore. All festivals include kayaking, interactive environmental education, children's activities, music, and food. For more information go to www.hrwa.org/ghrp/index.html.

October

Annual Connecticut River Source to Sea Cleanup

This four-state river cleanup offers many opportunities for participation. See how you can help by calling the CT River Watershed Council, (413) 772-2020, or go to www.ctriver .org for exact dates each year.

Annual Hudson River Estuary Snapshot Day: A Day in the Life of the Hudson River

This event provides a unique opportunity for school groups to join with environmental educators for an exploration of their section of the Hudson River, and then to tie those sections together to create a better understanding of the whole Hudson River estuary. A teacher workshop is often offered. For more information contact Steve Stanne, Interpretive Specialist, Hudson River Estuary Program, NYS Department of Environmental Conservation, 21 South Putt Corners Road, New Paltz, NY 12561 or at (845) 256-3077.

December

Christmas Ship Parade

Annual parade of ships on the Columbia and Willamette rivers. The Christmas Ship Fleet averages 55 to 60 boats between the two fleets. Both fleets will be out every night for two weeks in December. For more information visit www.christmasships.org/Columbia.htm or call (503) 275-9795.

Glossary

~~~~~~~~~~~~~~~~~~~~~~

acid rain: rainfall created from emissions released during the burning of fossil fuels that is mixed with sulfuric, nitric, and other acids to create a pH of less than 7.0

amphibian: a class of cold-blooded animals that begin life in the water as tadpoles with gills and develop lungs later, including frogs, salamanders, toads, and newts

anadromous: fish that migrate from saltwater to freshwater to spawn

bosque: the low-lying cottonwood forest adjacent to a river

channel: the deeper part of a river

catadromous: fish that migrate from freshwater to salt water to spawn

condensation: water droplets formed when water vapor rises and cools

delta: a deposit of sand and soil formed at the mouth of some rivers

erosion: worn away by water, wind, or some other means

estuary: where a river meets an ocean

evaporation: water turns into vapor and rises into the air

fisheries: established areas where fish are caught

flyway: a migration path used by birds

headwaters: the starting place or source of a river

hydroelectricity: producing electricity by water power

PCB: an abbreviation for Polychlorinated Biphenyls, mixtures of dangerous compounds that have been used as coolants and lubricants in transformers, capacitors, and other electrical equipment

petroglyph: a prehistoric rock carving

precipitation: rain, sleet, snow, or hail

riprap: debris that builds up behind a dam wall including sticks, gravel, and dirt

river: a large stream of water that flows in a bed or channel and empties into another body of water

salinity: measurement of salt dissolved in water

sediment: the minerals, leaves, and other items that flow into a river and settle on the bottom

spawn: to produce or deposit eggs

turbine: a device for converting the flow of water or other matter into mechanical motion that produces electricity

transpiration: process by which water is absorbed into the roots of a plant, moves through the plant, passes through pores in the leaves, and then evaporates into the air in the form of vapor

tundra: a treeless ecosystem mainly in the north polar areas where lichens, mosses, and some woody plants grow

underfur: thick, soft fur that grows under the longer, coarser hair

watershed: the area of land where all the water that drains off it or under it goes to the river

white water: the frothy water that is found in river rapids or waterfalls

Index

Learn More About the Beauty of the Natural World with These Books by Nancy Castaldo

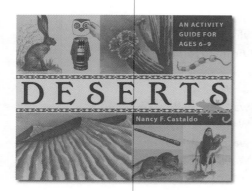

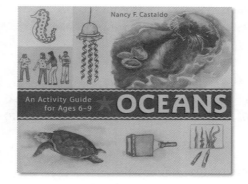

Deserts

An Activity Guide for Ages 6–9

By Nancy F. Castaldo

Introducing children to the wild and often misunderstood environment of the desert and the people and cultures that thrive in and around them. Filled with engaging activities and ideas on how children can help protect these delicate environments.

Illustrated throughout

$14.95 (CAN $22.95) 1-55652-524-9

Oceans

An Activity Guide for Ages 6–9

By Nancy F. Castaldo

* A selection of the Primary Teacher's Book Club

"Using fun activities and games, *Oceans* brilliantly underscores the connection that kids have with the oceans."

—Barbara Jeanne Polo, executive director, American Oceans Campaign

Illustrated throughout

$14.95 (CAN $22.95) 1-55652-443-9

Rainforests

An Activity Guide for Ages 6–9

By Nancy F. Castaldo

Rainforest-inspired activities introduce children to plants, animals, and people that contribute to the beauty of these forests, and encourage young readers to become active defenders of the rainforests no matter where they live.

Illustrated throughout

$14.95 (CAN $22.95) 1-55652-476-5

CHICAGO REVIEW PRESS

Distributed by
Independent Publishers Group
www.ipgbook.com

www.chicagoreviewpress.com

Available at your favorite bookstore or by calling (800) 888-4741